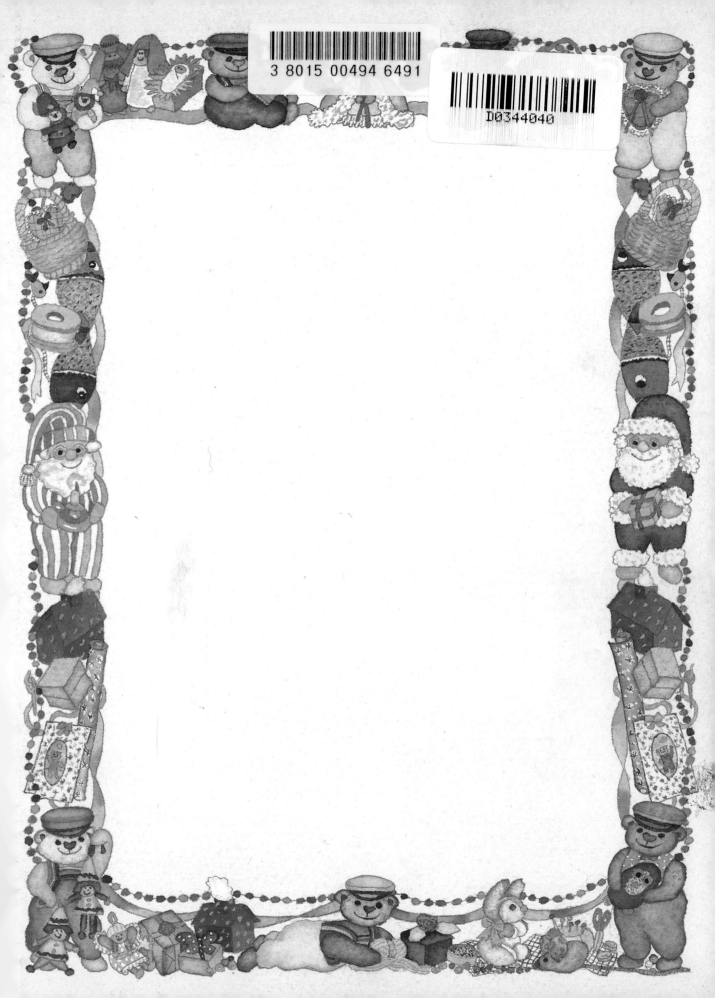

The Christmas Stocking Gift Book

Valerie Janitch

A DAVID & CHARLES CRAFT BOOK

British Library Cataloguing in Publication Data
Janitch, Valerie
    The Christmas stocking gift book. – (A David & Charles
craft book).
    1. Gifts. Making
    I. Title.
    745.5

    ISBN 0-7153-9335-9

Typeset by ABM (Typographics) Ltd, Hull
and printed in Italy
by New Interlitho SpA, Milan
for David & Charles Publishers plc
Brunel House Newton Abbot Devon

Distributed in the United States by
Sterling Publishing Co. Inc.
387 Park Avenue South, New York, NY 10016-8810

CONTENTS

My thanks . . .

Once again, very specially to Melvin Grey – for creating and furnishing Santa's workshop – and then for telling the Christmas Stocking Bears' story so beautifully with his enchanted photography.

To my editor, Vivienne Wells, for all her help and guidance – and for being specially supportive when I needed it.

To Pat Mobbs for all her help – especially with the bears.

To Sheila Barnett – without whom there might never have been a Christmas Mouse .

And, of course, to Becky Osborne, for all her enthusiasm.

**Details of other books and patterns by
Valerie Janitch can be obtained by writing to her at:
15 Ledway Drive, Wembley Park, Middlesex HA9 9TH.
Please enclose a stamped self-addressed envelope.**

CHRISTMAS STOCKING GIFTS ARE SPECIAL
Whether they're for pleasure or profit

The nicest things come in small packages, so they say, which explains why the kind of gifts that you find in your Christmas stocking are always so exciting.

The Christmas Stocking Gift Book *sets out to give you a whole range of gift ideas for the entire family, whatever their age and interests. The criteria of each basic design are a) that no matter whether it is something practical, a child's plaything, or just a bit of nonsense, it must be colourful and very attractive; b) that it doesn't take too long to make (bearing in mind how busy you are at this time of year); c) that nothing is beyond the ability and experience of any average craftsperson; d) that it is either very inexpensive – or else it doesn't cost much to make; e) that the basic design lends itself to many forms of adaptation and individual interpretation; and finally, f) that, of course, it is small enough to fit comfortably inside anyone's Christmas stocking.*

Add all that up, and any perceptive sales-minded reader will also recognise a happy hunting ground for attractive items with maximum profit-potential. Whether you are making things for fund-raising events, or to augment your own personal income, The Christmas Stocking Gift Book *should provide an invaluable source of inspiration and basic material.*

And remember, there are no copyright restrictions, provided you are making the things personally, and in reasonably limited quantities. (To protect yourself, and also add a professional touch to your work, it is a good idea to attach a small tag, saying 'Made by . . . . from an original design by Valerie Janitch'.)

But wait! Just like Christmas Day itself, there's more to come. To give you something else to think about while you stitch and glue, there's an amusing little story about the seven Christmas Stocking Bears who make the gifts for Santa Claus to put in the stockings. The illustrations follow the chain of events in Santa's workshop leading up to midnight on one rather special Christmas Eve. And if, along the way, you fall in love with Santa or the bears – you'll find full instructions for making them as well.

Naturally the Christmas Stocking itself can't be forgotten. You must have something to put everything in. There's a basic pattern to decorate as you please – and it needn't cost you a penny.

And to end the bears' story, and make your Christmas complete, there's an enchanting Nativity scene for you to enjoy and make.

THE BEST WAY . . .
Making life easier – and advice on materials and methods

There's a right way and a wrong way – which is an old adage that bears scrutiny. Because there's often a simpler way to do a difficult operation – or a way of by-passing it – or a little trick that makes a task easier – or even a way of cheating!

Sometimes it's just a question of finding the right piece of equipment or using a certain kind of glue. Remember, you don't have to obey any rules in this book, because there aren't any. All the instructions describe how to do things in the easiest and most direct way to achieve a successful result – even if they're not the 'correct' methods you're accustomed to. So use your common sense. And if you find an easier route that gets you there in the end . . . take it.

With all this in mind, you may like to share a few personal 'wrinkles'. Here they are, together with some general notes on the materials and methods that are used regularly throughout the book.

Ordinary household *greaseproof paper* is not only much cheaper, but also easier to use, than proper tracing paper.

To *transfer a pattern* to card or paper, trace it first onto greaseproof paper, then rub over the back with a soft pencil; fix this side flat on your card and retrace the lines with a firm point (ballpoint pen, hard pencil or knitting needle). Remove the trace, and a clear outline should remain on the card. (For patterns traced onto folded paper, turn the tracing over and trace your original outline through onto the other side before opening it up.)

When a pattern piece is marked 'reverse', turn it over to cut the second piece. Check to ensure that stripes, checks, etc, match equally on both pieces.

A sheet of *graph paper* or squared paper is very useful for copying patterns from diagrams; just fix your tracing paper on top and use your ruler to draw the lines following the measurements on the diagram.

Don't cut *fur fabric* with big scissors; use small, sharp, pointed ones – and only cut the jersey back of the fabric, *not* the fur.

Well-sharpened *scissors* make so much difference; a large pair for cutting out, and smaller, pointed ones for all the other jobs (except cutting paper; try to keep a separate pair for this, to prevent blunting your good ones).

Darning needles do a lot more than darn socks especially if you're making soft toys. They are invaluable for moving stuffing around or pulling it into a narrow point from the outside, and also for sewing heads and limbs to bodies, or taking very big stitches to sew on a doll's hair.

Tweezers are another non-essential item which nevertheless comes in useful over and over again. A quite small pair will make gluing on tiny beads and sequins really easy.

When choosing *fabrics* for small items, look for firmly and evenly woven cotton or cotton-blend or cotton-type materials. Avoid silky, man-made fabrics, and also thick or knobbly ones; both will fray and be difficult to sew.

Always sew with the *wrong sides together*, unless otherwise instructed.

Seam allowances are indicated for each individual design.

Bulky *hems* can ruin a dainty garment on a small toy. Cut your fabric along the thread, then turn the hem under and herringbone stitch neatly over the raw edge.

Buying cheap *felt* is a false economy: it will stretch and pull when you sew it – especially if it is subsequently stuffed. Choose a good quality, which is smooth and firm, and of an even thickness all over. Press oversewn (overcast) seams flat with your fingernail.

Very *narrow braids* are often hard to find. But some lampshade and dress braids can be cut down the centre to make two separate lengths half the width of the original. When you examine it carefully, you will see that a fine thread connects the two sides of the braid; if you cut along this, they come apart completely undamaged.

When a length of tiny *pearl bead trimming* is called for, don't buy a box and thread your own. If you buy them by the metre (or yard), they're all firmly fixed to the string – avoiding a cascade of tiny pearls rolling all over the floor.

Very *small felt circles* are often needed – especially for eyes. It is far easier to cut them accurately if you mark them directly onto the felt. Find something with a circular rim the size you require – a thimble, the top from a pill container, pen cap, etc – the sharper the edge the better. Rub a contrasting wax crayon, lead pencil, felt-tip pen or chalk liberally over the rim. Press down onto the felt; then, still pressing firmly, twist it like a pastry cutter, taking care not to move the position. Lift

off and cut along the marked line with sharp scissors. Alternatively, find – or cut – a self-adhesive label the size of the circle you require: press it lightly down onto your felt, then cut round it. Remove the label carefully.

Some toys have their heads sewn on with *ladder stitch*. This is simple to do. First fix the head in position as instructed, and, beginning at the back, make a stitch in the body, where you want the head to join it; then take your thread straight up and make a stitch in the head; take your thread straight down to make another stitch in the body – and up to make another stitch in the head. The thread between the stitches forms the ladder.

Some of the little figures have *heads* made from turned paper balls. These are great fun to use – and even more time-saving if you can find flesh-tinted ones; if you can't, paint them with flesh poster colour. When you draw the *features*, try using sepia ink – or a sepia water-colour pencil; it gives a softer and more attractive effect than black.

A clear, quick-drying *all-purpose adhesive* will do most gluing jobs. UHU has a long nozzle, which can be very useful when applying glue. In some cases a *dry stick glue* is recommended; this is ideal for sticking paper, or when you want to cover card with thin fabric, because there is no danger of the glue seeping through and staining the fabric. Some glue-sticks are suitable only for paper, so if you need it for fabric, make sure it is listed on the outside (UHU Stic is a good one).

MEASUREMENTS

Use either metric or imperial measurements, but don't compare the two because they are often different. To make the instructions as simple as possible for you, each design has been worked out individually in both metric and imperial, and the nearest most practical measurement is always given. It is most important, therefore, that you use one set of measurements only.

When the direction of measurements is not specifically stated, the depth is given first, followed by the width – ie: 10 x 20cm (4 x 8in) = 10cm (4in) deep x 20cm (8in) wide.

SAFETY STANDARDS

New regulations which implement a European Directive have tightened up the safety standards regarding toys to be sold in the UK. While the new Regulations do not apply in a situation where toys are made to be given for example to organisations such as a church or an association for sale at a fete to raise funds, they do apply to small businesses and those charities and organisations who make or offer toys for sale in the course of a business on a regular basis. These toys must comply with the European safety standards and should carry a 'CE' mark to certify that they do so.

However, it is not necessary to have expensive tests done on your work. Provided that a toy has been manufactured in accordance with British Standards 5665 you can self-certify your toys. You could obtain a declaration from the suppliers of materials, fillings, paints etc that their products meet the required safety standards. If you are satisfied that you have used safe, tested materials and that the toy has been well made with eg facial features securely fixed, there is no reason why you cannot 'self-certify' your own toys. The 'CE' labels can be obtained from suppliers of materials which meet the required safety standards.

MY THANKS

For all the beautiful ribbons: to C. M. Offray & Son Ltd, Fir Tree Place, Church Road, Ashford, Middlesex TW15 2PH (07842 47281/2/3) and 261 Madison Avenue, New York, NY 10016 ([212] 682-8010).

For specially colour co-ordinated patchwork fabrics, velvet tubing, turned paper craft balls, cream felt, Vilene Bondaweb and all embroidery materials: to Artisan, 22 High Street, Pinner, Middlesex HA5 5PW (01-866 0327).

For fur fabrics, fillings and all other soft toy making materials: to Dainty Toys, Unit 35, Phoenix Road, Crowther Industrial Estate (District 3), Washington, Tyne and Wear NE38 0AB (091 416 7886/417 6277).

For all the gift-wrap papers and gift-ties: to Hallmark Limited, Hallmark House, Station Road, Henley-on-Thames, Oxon RG9 1LQ (0491 578383).

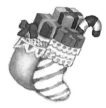

FINISHING TOUCHES
Trimmings are the icing on the cake

The wealth of gift ideas in the following pages ranges from dainty dolls and cuddly toys through specs and pencil cases to picture frames and tea cosies. But a large proportion have one important factor in common: they are completed with some kind of trimming that immediately picks them out to make them individual and 'special'.

High quality trimmings with that 'touch of class' are often expensive. But you *can* make them yourself – without any danger of your work looking 'amateur' or 'home-made' in the disparaging sense of those terms. Top-quality Offray ribbons make sure your trimmings still have that professional look – without breaking the bank.

Here is a collection of 'finishing touches' . . . most of which you will notice throughout the book.

PLAITED BRAID

Offray ribbons come in a wonderful range of colours and subtle shades, and if you plait together three lengths of their 1.5mm (¹⁄₁₆in) wide satin, you can always make an attractive narrow braid in just the shade you want. Or you could plait two or three different ribbons for a multi-coloured braid.

1 The directions for the item that you are making will usually tell you how much ribbon you need to make the length of braid you require. For instance: 'Make a plait from three 25cm (10in) lengths of 1.5mm (¹⁄₁₆in) ribbon.' In this case, if you are making the braid in one colour only, cut one 25cm (10in) length of ribbon and one 50cm (20in) length. Fold the longer piece in half, smear a trace of glue inside the fold, place one end of the shorter piece between the fold, then pinch together (figure a).

PLAITED BRAID

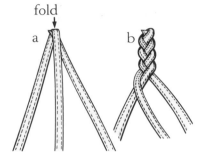

fold

a   b

2 Push a pin through the folded end and secure it to a drawing-board or something similar. Then begin to plait very evenly, making sure that the strands of ribbon are always flat – never fold them over. Keep the ribbon taut and draw the plait very firmly between your fingertips every 2 to 3cm (inch or so) to make it smooth and even (figure b). Hold the ends together with a paper-clip.

3 Glue the braid into place, spreading the glue just beyond the point where you intend to cut it, to ensure that it does not unravel. Press the cut ends down well, adding a little more glue if necessary.

4 If you are not following directions, you can calculate the amount of ribbon needed by measuring the length of braid you require and adding a third (then multiply by three for the total amount). For example, if you need a 30cm (12in) length of braid, plait three pieces of ribbon 40cm (16in) long. Which means you will need to buy 1.2m (48in or 1³⁄₈yd) of ribbon. If you want to make a multi-colour braid in two or three toning shades, calculate the amount of ribbon you will need in each colour accordingly.

RIBBON BOWS

The formal bow is extremely elegant, and looks wonderful in a wide satin or gauzy ribbon. The butterfly bow is quick, easy, and very dainty: single-face satin is best, in any width.

Formal Ribbon Bows

1 Fold under the cut ends of a piece of ribbon, so that they overlap at the centre back (figure a).

2 Gather the centre (figure b) and draw up, binding tightly several times with your thread to hold it securely (figure c).

3 Fold a scrap of ribbon lengthways into three and bind it closely around the centre: secure the ends at the back and trim off the surplus (figure d).

4 Gather across the centre of another piece of ribbon, then draw up tightly and fold it around (as figure e) for the ties (streamers).

5 Stitch the ties behind the bow and trim the cut ends in an inverted V-shape (figure f).

RIBBON BOWS

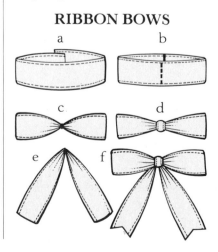

a   b

c   d

e   f

Butterfly Bows

1 Cut a piece of single-face satin ribbon (the directions will tell you the width and the length). On the wrong side, mark point A at the centre, close to the lower edge (figure g). On the right side, mark dots for points B on the top edge – see your individual directions for the distance points B should be from A. Then trim the cut ends in an inverted V-shape as figure h.

2 Hold the ribbon with the wrong side facing you. Using closely matching thread, bring your needle through point A from the back, close to the edge of the ribbon. Then curve the ends around and bring the needle through each point B. Draw up so that both points B are over point A (figure i).

3 Make tiny gathering stitches up from points B to C (figure j). Take your thread over the top edge of the bow and gather right down from point C to point D. Draw up neatly, then wind the thread tightly around three or four times and secure at the back so that the result resembles figure k.

TINY TASSELS

A quickie novelty trimming made from the very narrowest ribbon; the result is surprisingly smart.

1 Take a length of 1.5mm (¹/₁₆in) wide ribbon and fold it as figure a – the length and number of folds determine the size of the tassel.

TINY TASSELS

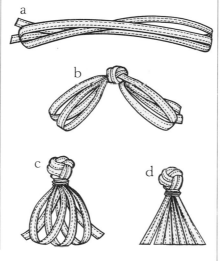

2 Hold the folded ends neatly together and absolutely level (figure a), then make a knot at the centre (figure b). Take the two sides down so that all the ends are together, then bind very tightly with matching thread close under the knot (figure c).

3 Snip off the folded ends and trim neatly to length (figure d).

SATIN ROSES

Artificial flowers – even the most unrealistic and poorly made ones – are always expensive. And the most popular flower of all, the romantic rose, is usually the *most* expensive. So why not make your own from a length of satin ribbon?

You'll be surprised at your own ingenuity when you produce your first rose. They can be anything from miniature to life-size, from bud to full bloom; and of course, you can match nature to exquisite perfection from the Offray ribbon shade card.

The width of the ribbon determines the size of the flower; the longer the ribbon, the more petals it will have. The directions will indicate the width and length that you should use for the design. Use single-face satin ribbon (except for miniature 3mm [¹/₈in] roses).

1 Cut a length of ribbon as directed. Fold the corner as the broken line on figure a and bring point A down to meet point B as figure b. Fold again as the broken line on figure b and bring point C over point A to meet point B as figure c. (Omit the second fold for 3mm [¹/₈in] ribbon.)

2 Roll the ribbon round four times, with the folded corner inside, to form a tight tube, and make a few stitches through the base to hold (figure d). This forms the centre of the rose.

3 To make the petals, fold the ribbon down so that the edge is aligned with the tube (figure e), then curve the ribbon around to form a cone, keeping the top of the tube level with

BUTTERFLY BOWS

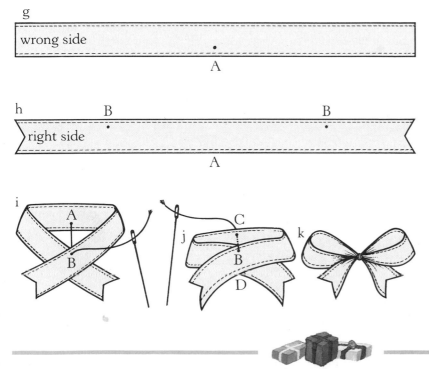

g

wrong side

A

h   B   B

> right side

A

i

A

B

j   C

B

D

k

SATIN ROSES

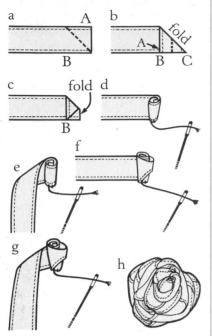

the diagonal fold. When the tube again lies parallel to the remaining ribbon, make two or three stitches at the base to hold the petal you have just made (figure f).

4 Continue to make petals with the remainder of the ribbon, sewing each one to the base of the flower before you start the next (figure g). Shape the rose as you work by gradually making the petals a little more open.

5 Finish the cut end neatly underneath the base of the completed rose (figure h).

RIBBON LEAVES

Sometimes the trimming itself needs a finishing touch; in the case of a flower – especially the satin roses – a leaf can set it off to perfection. These take only a moment to make; use Spring Moss green satin ribbon, or gold or silver metallic grosgrain ribbon. Have the ribbon a little wider than your proposed leaves.

1 For a satin leaf, cut off a length of single-face satin ribbon *twice* the length of your proposed leaf, plus 2cm

(¾in). Spread clear adhesive on the back of the ribbon with your fingertip, to cover *half* the length; then fold the ribbon in half with the glue inside and smooth over to flatten and ensure that the two pieces are firmly stuck. Cut out the leaf shape with sharp scissors.

2 For a gold or silver metallic grosgrain leaf, cut off a piece of ribbon a little more than the length of your proposed leaf. Spread clear adhesive over one side, rubbing it in well with your fingertip. When it is dry, cut out the leaf shape with sharp scissors. If the grosgrain ribbon is wide enough, turn your pattern so that the horizontal weave of the ribbon runs diagonally across the leaf: this looks very attractive, and also makes the leaf curl realistically.

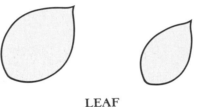

**LEAF
PATTERNS**

WOOLLY POMPONS

The final finishing touch that everyone loves, and wants at one time or another – from Santa Claus to baby bunnies. You *can* buy them from craft shops but they're nearly always better if you make them yourself.

The directions are always the same, but the size of your card circle determines the size of your ball. This pattern makes a trimmed pompon about 4cm (1½in) in diameter. For a larger or smaller pompon, simply adjust the size of the pattern.

WOOLLY POMPON

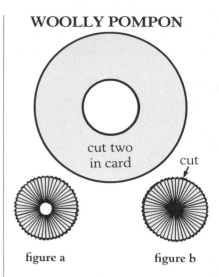

figure a   figure b

You Will Need:
Knitting yarn: avoid anything *very* thick or thin or heavily textured
Strong thread or fine string (if your yarn is not strong, see step 3)
Thin card
A large tapestry needle
Small pointed scissors

1 Cut two circles of card as the pattern. Fold a 4m (4yd) length of yarn into four and thread a tapestry needle (have fewer strands if your yarn is thicker). Place the two card circles together and wrap the yarn evenly over and over them as figure a, continuing until the central hole is full (figure b).

2 Push pointed scissors through the yarn and between the two card circles (see the arrow on figure b). Cut the yarn all round (keeping your scissors between the card).

3 Slip a 20cm (8in) length of double yarn between the two layers of card to surround the yarn in the centre; knot together, pulling as tight as you can (use thread or string if yarn is weak).

4 Cut away the card, then trim the pompon severely (but not the ties) to make a neat, round, firm ball.

5 Use the ties to fix the pompon in place – or snip them off if not needed.

The Bears' Story

PART ONE

The seven Christmas Stocking Bears were seated at a round table in a corner of Santa's workshop, having their breakfast.

'Pass the marmalade,' whispered Greengage Bear, taking a slice of bread.

'Honey's nicer,' whispered Tangerine Bear, scraping the pot.

'Don't talk with your mouth full,' whispered Banana Bear, pushing the marmalade across the table.

The bears were whispering because Santa Claus always had a lie-in on Christmas Eve, so that he was ready for the long night ahead, riding through the sky on his sleigh. But the bears had to be up early, and now they all tip-toed quietly past his bed to their benches, where they were making the gifts to fill the Christmas stockings.

Tangerine Bear got to work quickly on his little people. There was still a lot to do and, like everyone else, he had to be finished by midnight.

TANGERINE BEAR'S
Christmas Stocking Gifts

Traditional Christmas characters come in pairs, making it difficult to choose between choirboys and angels, fairies and pixies . . . or demure little snowmaidens well wrapped up to beat the winter frosts. They have dual roles, too; tuck them into a stocking – or hang them on the tree.

ONE-PLUS-ONE MAKES PARTNERS

Equally charming as stocking fillers or hanging on the tree, these animated little figures are all variations on an incredibly simple theme, using velvet tubing – which is made by the ribbon people, Offray. Having stiffened and shaped the tubing with pipe cleaners or chenille stems pushed through the centre, just add wooden beads for the hands and feet, and a craft ball head.

Create a hairstyle from embroidery wool or knitting yarn, and you are ready to dress your character in felt or fabric. Felt couldn't be simpler, of course. But you can use pretty, lightweight fabrics just as easily, after they have had some special treatment; back your chosen fabric with a plain one of similar weight by bonding them together. The bonding process prevents fraying, and you are left with a garment that you can sew or stick, just like felt.

The Basic Figure

MATERIALS
23cm (¼yd) Offray velvet tubing
2 pipe cleaners or chenille stems
Turned paper, or alternative, craft ball, 3cm (1¼in) diameter, flesh-tinted if possible, for head
2 natural wood beads for hands, 1cm (⅜in) diameter
2 coloured wood beads for feet, 1cm (⅜in) diameter
Twilley's stranded embroidery wool, or fine knitting yarn, for hair
10cm (4in) satin ribbon, 1.5mm (¹⁄₁₆in) wide, to hang
Tiny pin
Flesh-coloured poster paint (if ball is not coloured)
Black ball-point pen or ink
Clear adhesive

1 Cut the pipe cleaners (or chenille stems), and the velvet tubing, as follows:

	Pipe Cleaners	Velvet Tubing
Arms:	9cm (3½in)	7.5cm (3in)
Body:	7cm (2¾in)*	5.5cm (2⅛in)
Legs:	11cm (4¼in)	9.5cm (3¾in)

*Use remainder of above cleaner

2 Push the pieces of pipe cleaner through the tubing so that they protrude equally at each end; hold the inner cord to prevent it slipping, but if you accidentally lose the end, pull it right out and discard it.

3 Following the diagram, bend the body in half and glue the arms between (mark the centre of the arms

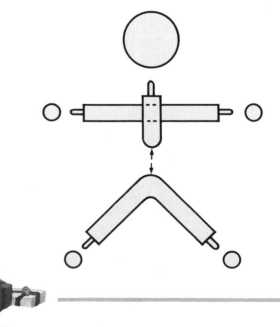

beforehand, to ensure they are exactly equal). Bend the legs as indicated.

4 Spread a little glue over each bend, as arrows, and leave for about five minutes. Then press the body and legs firmly together.

5 Glue the appropriate beads onto the ends of the pipe cleaners for the hands and feet.

6 Paint the ball if necessary, then examine it to choose the best surface for the face; indicate this with an arrow on top of the head. Glue the head onto the ends of the body pipe cleaner – *but check the individual directions first*, as you may need to delay this until the figure is dressed.

7 Follow the individual directions for the hairstyle. When you reach the final stage of trimming the wool to length, wrap a face tissue around the dressed figure, to protect the garments; if any bits *do* fall on the felt or fabric, brush them off with a stiff paintbrush.

8 When the figure is completely dressed and the hairstyle is finished, mark round dots for the eyes, a very short line for the nose, and a curve for the mouth if required, with a black (or very dark brown/sepia) pen.

9 Last of all, fold the ribbon in half and pin the cut ends to the top of the head, forming a loop.

Carolling Choirboys

MATERIALS
Basic figure as above
10cm (4in) square of felt to match velvet tubing, for cassock
8cm (3¼in) square of white felt for surplice
40cm (16in) white lace, 10mm (⅜in) deep
Matching threads
Scrap of stiff coloured paper
Scrap of thin white paper

1 Make up the basic figure in wine or forest green velvet tubing, with black shoes, but don't glue the head on yet.

2 Cut the cassock (page 16) in matching felt. Oversew (overcast) the straight edges to form the centre back seam and turn to the right side. Fit on the figure and join the front to the back over each shoulder.

3 Cut the surplice in white felt. Stitch lace behind the lower edge, easing gently round the curve. Oversew the centre back seam and turn to the right side. Fit the surplice and join over the shoulders, as cassock.

4 Glue the head on firmly.

5 Gather the remaining lace close to the straight edge, then draw up tightly around the neck and join at the back.

6 Cut forty 7.5cm (3in) lengths of wool: tie loosely with a single strand 3cm (1¼in) from one end, then glue the tied area to the top of the head so that the shorter end overlaps the forehead and the other hangs down at the back.
  Cut twenty-four 10cm (4in) lengths of wool and tie loosely at the centre with a single strand. Glue over the top of the head across the first piece, to hang down at each side.
  Trim neatly to length all round, as illustrated.

7 Fold a 2 x 3.5cm (¾ x 1⅜in) piece of coloured paper in half for the music cover; letter *Carols* on the front. Cut a piece of thin white paper fractionally smaller, fold in half and glue the *fold* inside the fold of the cover, to make the pages. Glue to the hands, as illustrated.

Very Young Fairies

MATERIALS
Basic figure as above
9cm (3½in) square of spotted voile (dotted Swiss), or alternative, for dress
Sufficient lightweight plain white fabric to back voile
Iron-on bonding material (Vilene Bondaweb or Pellon Wunder-Under)
55cm (24in) lace, 10mm (⅜in) deep, to match dress
Thread to match lace
Silver or gold flower sequin, 12-13mm (½in) diameter
Tiny sequin stars
Stiff coloured paper for wings
Toothpick

1 Make up the basic figure in velvet tubing to match your dress fabric, and glue on the head.

2 Trace the dress onto Bondaweb (Wunder-Under) and bond voile (or alternative) onto the backing fabric and cut out, as instructed.

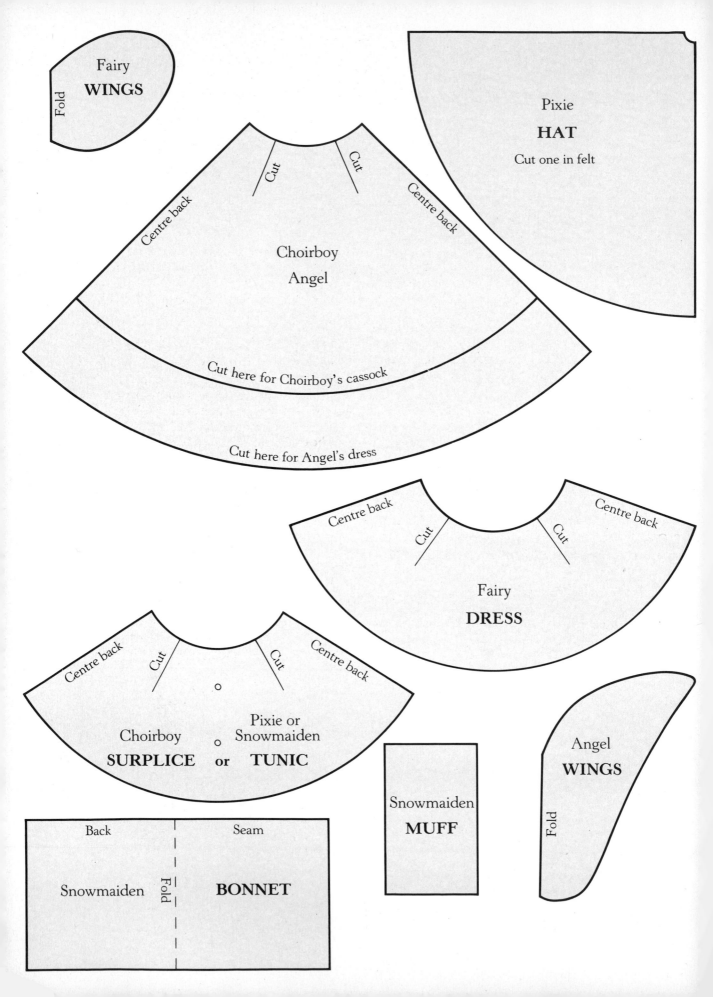

Fairy
WINGS

Fold

Pixie
HAT

Cut one in felt

Centre back

Centre back

Cut

Cut

Choirboy

Angel

Cut here for Choirboy's cassock

Cut here for Angel's dress

Centre back

Centre back

Cut

Cut

Fairy
DRESS

Centre back

Centre back

Cut

Cut

Choirboy
SURPLICE **or**

Pixie or
Snowmaiden
TUNIC

Snowmaiden
MUFF

Angel
WINGS

Fold

Back

Seam

Snowmaiden

Fold

BONNET

3 Overlap the straight edges 2-3mm (⅛in) and glue the join.

4 Gather 40cm (18in) lace; pin evenly around the hem, then draw up to fit and stitch into place.

Fit the dress on the figure and glue the top edge across the body and shoulders to hold it in place.

5 Gather 15cm (6in) lace and draw up around the neck for the collar.

6 Cut forty 9cm (3½in) lengths of wool; tie loosely with a single strand 3cm (1¼in) from one cut end, then glue the tied area to the top of the head so that one end overlaps the forehead and the other hangs down at the back.

Cut twenty-four 12cm (4¾in) lengths of wool and tie loosely at the centre with a single strand. Glue over the top of the head across the first piece, to hang down at each side.

Trim neatly to length all round, as illustrated.

7 Glue sequin stars at random over the hair.

8 Cut the wings in folded coloured paper.

Spread glue along the fold and glue to the back of the figure.

9 Cut the toothpick to measure 3.5cm (1⅜in) and glue the flower sequin to the tip. Then glue the other end to the fairy's hand.

Christmas Angels

MATERIALS
Basic figure as above
12 x 20cm (5 x 8in) lightweight fabric for dress and wings
12cm (5in) square of lightweight plain white fabric to back dress
Iron-on bonding material (Vilene Bondaweb or Pellon Wunder-Under)
70cm (⅞yd) very narrow white lace
30cm (12in) tiny pearl bead trimming
Stiff white paper

1 Make up the basic figure in velvet tubing to match your dress fabric, and glue on the head.

2 Trace the dress onto Bondaweb (Wunder-Under) and bond your patterned fabric onto the backing fab-

ric. Do the same with the wings, but back with paper instead of fabric.

3 Overlap the straight edges of the dress 2-3mm (⅛in) and glue the join.

Glue the narrow lace around the hem to overlap the lower edge. Glue a row of pearls immediately above, with the straight edge of another band of lace above the pearls.

4 Fit the dress on the figure and glue the top edge across the body and shoulders to hold it in place.

5 Glue lace around the neck to form a stand-up collar, with a row of pearls on top.

6 Take six 76cm (30in) strands of wool and fold them into four; tie the centre of the 'skein' loosely with a single strand. Glue the tied centre to the top of the head, then bring each side down smoothly over the face and round to the back, gluing lightly to hold in place; cross the two pieces at the back of the neck, then take the ends up to cover the back of the head, ending on top behind the tied centre. Tuck in, or trim off, any untidy ends.

Fold two more strands into eight; twist slightly, then tie in a loose knot, tucking the ends underneath before you glue it to the crown of the angel's head, over the ends of the first skein.

7 Circle the bun with pearls, gluing the ends at the back.

8 Glue lace behind the cut edge of the wings so that it overlaps as illustrated. Then glue to the back of the figure, the lowest point of the wings 5cm (2in) above the hem of the dress, curving them back behind the head.

Fir-Tree Pixies

MATERIALS
Basic figure as above
15cm (6in) square of felt to tone with velvet tubing, for tunic and hat
30cm (12in) narrow black ric-rac braid
2 tiny silver beads for buttons
Matching threads

1 Make up the basic figure in velvet tubing, and glue on the head.

2 Cut the tunic and hat once each in felt; choose a lighter shade which tones, but contrasts with the darker velvet.

3 Stitch silver beads to right side of tunic at points marked o.
    Oversew (overcast) the straight edges of the tunic to form the centre back seam, then turn to the right side.
    Stitch ric-rac braid around the lower edge of the tunic.
    Fit tunic on figure and join the front to the back over each shoulder.

4 Follow the directions for the Choirboy (step 6) for the hairstyle.

5 Oversew the straight edges of the hat to form the centre back seam, and turn to the right side.
    Stitch ric-rac braid around the lower edge.
    Spread adhesive around the inner edge and glue to the head.

6 To hang (Basic Figure – step 9), stitch loop to point of hat.

Little Snowmaidens

MATERIALS
Basic figure as above
10cm (4in) square of matching felt for tunic
Thread to match felt
Small amount of fairly fine knitting yarn in a contrasting colour

1 Make up the basic figure in velvet tubing, and glue on the head.

2 Cut the tunic in felt.
    Oversew (overcast) the straight edges to form the centre back seam, then turn to the right side.
    Fit tunic on figure and join the front to the back over each shoulder.

3 Follow the directions for the Fairy (step 6) for the hairstyle.

4 Using fine knitting needles and fairly fine yarn, knit in plain garter stitch a piece 4cm (1½in) wide x 8cm (3in) long, for the bonnet (place your knitting over the pattern to check measurements).
    Fold in half as indicated by the broken line, and join the centre back seam.
    Gather round the lower edge with a length of yarn, then fit the bonnet on the head and draw up around the neck, stitching the front corners together under the chin.

5 Knit another piece for the muff, 2.5cm (1in) wide x 4cm (1½in) long (check measurements against the pattern, as before).
    Join the two short ends, then turn to the right side and fit the muff over the hands.

The Bears' Story

PART TWO

Greengage Bear carefully wound a length of fluffy grey yarn around a pencil, measured and cut it. He was making a beard for one of his gnomes, and he thought grey would look good with the soft pink felt he had chosen for the gnome's suit.

Holding the pencil carefully he reached for his tube of glue. But it wasn't where he thought it was. He looked all over his work-bench.

'Has anyone borrowed my glue?' he called to the others in an accusing voice. The bears had a rule about never borrowing without asking first.

'It's that Christmas Mouse again,' exploded Tangerine Bear. 'It's been stealing my felt and ribbons.'

Damson Bear smiled sympathetically and threw his own tube of glue across: 'Borrow mine,' he offered.

'Thanks,' said Greengage Bear gratefully. 'But I'm still going to tell Santa.'

GREENGAGE BEAR'S
Christmas Stocking Gifts

Whiskery gnomes in colourful suits with bells on their pointed hats: a lucky find in anyone's stocking . . . or an amusing party table decoration. And the smartest photograph frames – in a variety of designs to please every member of the family.

SEVEN WHISKERY GNOMES

Roll up some paper, cover it with felt, add a ball for the head, a magnificent set of woolly whiskers, a pair of arms and a pointed hat . . . and you've nearly finished an amusing mascot or a fun table decoration. In either role, these dumpy little characters have lots of appeal – especially if you're hunting for small items to attract customers.

As you can see from the illustrations, it's the hair and whiskers that make the impact. So if you haven't any suitable coloured leftover bits of wool with interesting texture – beg, borrow or steal from your friends.

MATERIALS
20cm (8in) square of coloured felt
5 x 10cm (2 x 4in) black felt
5cm (2in) square of flesh felt
Table tennis or craft ball, 4cm (1½in) diameter
Knitting yarn (plain or textured, small amount, not too fine) in black, white, grey or brown
15cm (6in) single-face black satin ribbon, 6mm (¼in) wide
2 pipe cleaners (chenille stems)
Wooden bead, about 7mm (¼in) diameter (pink, red or purple) for the nose
Small bell for hat
16 x 25cm (6 x 10in) cartridge paper
Cooking foil
8cm (3in) square of thin card
7.5 x 10cm (3 x 4in), and two 2cm (¾in) circles, stiff card
Matching threads
Flesh-colour poster paint
Black fibre-tip pen or black ink
Pencil
Adhesive tape
Clear adhesive

1 Cut a 4cm (1½in) diameter hole in the centre of the square of thin card.

2 Cut four 4 x 25cm (1½ x 10in) strips of cartridge paper. Roll one up and place it inside the hole, allowing it to open out fully so that it fits snugly. Mark the overlap, then carefully remove the cylinder of paper and glue the join, keeping the cut edges exactly level.

Roll up another strip of paper and put it inside the first one, allowing it to open up to fit closely against the sides, cut edges level (add a spot of glue to hold it in place). Repeat with the remaining strips.

3 Cut a piece of coloured felt 7 x 13cm (2½ x 5in) for the suit; glue it around the body cylinder overlapping 1.5cm (½in) at the top and bottom. Turn this surplus neatly over the edge and glue inside.

4 Cut the hand four times in flesh felt. Cut a 12.5cm (5in) length of pipe cleaner (chenille stem) for the arms. Mark each end as shown on the arms' pattern, then glue the hands on as follows: spread glue over a hand piece and lower one end of the pipe cleaner down onto it in the correct position (check against the pattern), then add a spot more glue over the pipe cleaner before pressing the second hand piece down on top. Trim edges level if necessary.

5 Cut the sleeves' pattern once in coloured felt. Lay the arms on top, the hands protruding at each end, then roll the felt round the arms with a small overlap; pin, and then slip-stitch the join.

6 Mark the centre of the arms and match to the centre back of the body, then curve the arms round the body,

20

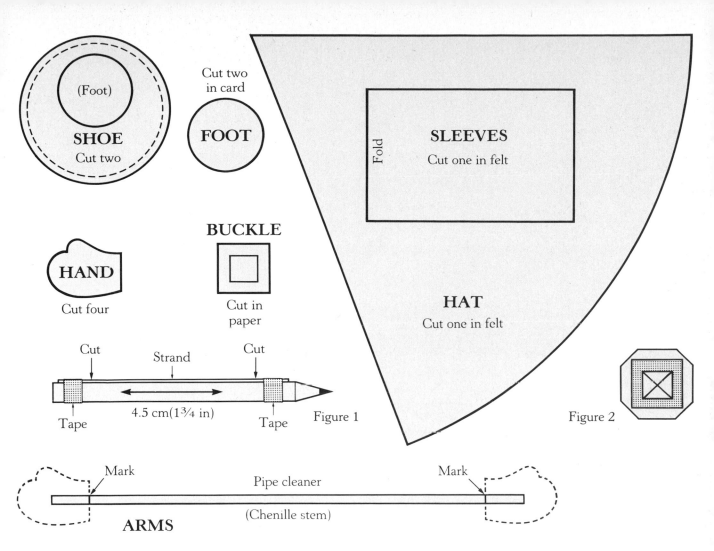

SHOE Cut two
(Foot)

FOOT Cut two in card

HAND Cut four

BUCKLE Cut in paper

SLEEVES Cut one in felt
Fold

HAT Cut one in felt

Cut — Strand — Cut

Tape — 4.5 cm (1¾ in) — Tape — Figure 1

Figure 2

Mark — Pipe cleaner — Mark

ARMS (Chenille stem)

with the join inside and thumbs facing up; oversew the top edge of the arms to the top edge of the body for about 3cm (1¼in) across the back.

7 Paint half the ball with poster colour for the face. When dry, spread glue liberally around the top edge of the body (towards the inside), then press the head well down into position.

8 Wind yarn evenly 10-15 times around the 7.5cm (3in) deep card. Slip off carefully and tie the centre loosely with a single strand, then cut the loops. Glue over the top of the head, overlapping the forehead and hanging down the back.

Wind more yarn 10-15 times around the 10cm (4in) deep card, slide off, tie and cut in the same way; then glue across the first piece, centres matching, so that it hangs down at each side.

9 To make the beard, cut a single strand of yarn about 12cm (5in) long: lay it along a pencil and tape the ends

to hold it taut (figure 1). Wind yarn closely and evenly (but quite loosely) 20-30 times around the centre of the pencil, to cover about 4.5cm (1¾in), as indicated. Then cut the single strand at one end, close to the tape: fold it back and glue it neatly over the coiled yarn, trimming off the excess. Repeat with the strand at the other end. Slide the beard off the pencil and glue around the lower part of the face, the centre level with the top of the body.

10 Cut the hat in coloured felt. Oversew the straight edges for the centre back join, then turn to the right side. Stitch a bell to the tip.

Fit a pipe cleaner inside, pushing it right up to the point and pinning it (from the outside) against the seam, about 1.5cm (½in) from the lower edge; cut off any excess.

Spread glue inside the lower edge of the hat and pull it down over the head as illustrated. When dry, remove the pin.

11 Trim the hair neatly all round.

12 Circle the body with the ribbon, about 1.5cm (½in) above the lower edge, gluing the join at the back.

13 To make his buckle, trace the pattern onto cartridge paper and cut out. Glue to the wrong side of the foil. Cut the outer edge of the foil as in figure 2; and cut a cross inside the centre of the buckle, as shown. Turn the outer and inner surplus neatly over to the back.

Glue the buckle over the centre front of the belt.

14 Cut the shoe twice in black felt. Gather close to the

edge with small stitches. Place a card foot on the wrong side of the felt, positioning it as indicated on the pattern, then draw up the gathers as tightly as possible and secure.

Spread adhesive over the gathered (back) area of each shoe and glue under the edge of the body, positioning as illustrated.

15 Glue bead nose to centre of face, resting on top of his beard.

16 Mark dots for eyes with fibre-tip pen or ink.

NINE FAMILY PHOTOGRAPH FRAMES

The frames in the illustration are intended merely to inspire you. You'll have endless ideas of your own – not only influenced by the photographs you plan to put inside, but also by the fabrics you find in your cuttings collection. The dimensions of all the frames illustrated are given for your guidance in visualising your own designs, and a 'materials and methods' description of each one follows the basic instructions.

If you plan to sell your frames, you might find it worth investing in a spray mounting adhesive; it's a rather expensive way to stick, but this kind of adhesive makes mounting down smoothly wonderfully easy.

You don't have to use gift-wrap to back the frames – any lightweight plain or patterned paper will do; but gift-wrap adds another professional touch.

MATERIALS
Stiff mounting board
Thin white card
Fabric to cover
Gift-wrap paper or lightweight paper to back
Braid, ribbon, pearl bead trimming, lace, etc
  (see individual descriptions of frames)
Purchased self-adhesive hook or ring fitting to hang *or* 10cm
  (4in) narrow ribbon for a free-standing frame
Paper towel (if necessary)
Dry-stick adhesive
Clear adhesive

1 Carefully measure and draw your frame on a piece of thin card, ruling lines very accurately or drawing circles with compasses.

2 Cut the card out and dry-stick it very smoothly to the back of your fabric. Cut the fabric 1.5cm (½in) from the outer edge of the card (figure 1).

3 Cut the fabric 1cm (⅜in) from the inner edge. For a circle, snip this surplus into tiny tabs (figure 2) and then fold them neatly over the edge and glue them to the back of the card (figure 3). For straight sides, snip the corners (figure 2), then fold the fabric neatly over the edge and glue to the back of the card (figure 3).

4 Glue on any decoration around the inner edge.

5 Cut a piece of mounting board the same size, but this time cut the inner hole or holes at least 5mm (¼in) larger all round – more if you have enough space on the mount without coming too close to the outer edge.

6 Glue this piece to the back of the thin card, edges absolutely level. Then snip the overlap on a circle into V-shaped tabs (figure 4) or mitre (cut off at an angle) the corners of a straight-sided overlap (figure 4). Turn the surplus over the edge of the card and glue it neatly to the back (figure 5).

7 Cover the back of the frame with plain paper or gift-wrap, cutting it just fractionally smaller. When it is dry, carefully cut away the paper covering the central hole, level with the cut edge of the backing card.

8 Glue braid around the outside, pulling it taut as you fold it over the outer edge. Or trim as suggested.

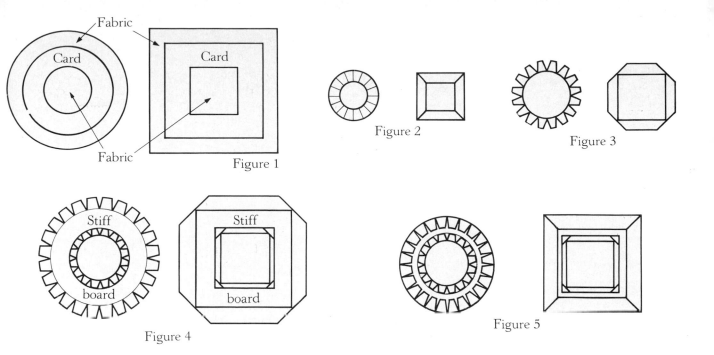

Figure 1

Figure 2

Figure 3

Figure 4

Figure 5

9 Cut your picture to size and fit it inside the frame, padding the back if necessary with pieces of paper towel. Then cover the back of the 'hole' with a piece of matching backing paper at least 1cm (3/8in) larger all round; glue it securely into place.

10 Fix purchased hook or ring/s to the back of the frame to hang.

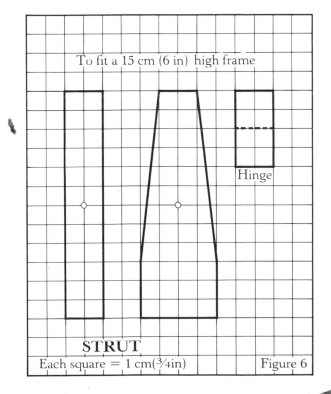

To fit a 15 cm (6 in) high frame

Hinge

STRUT

Each square = 1 cm(3/4in)　　　Figure 6

For a free-standing frame, cut two pieces of stiff board similar to figure 6, but adjusting the measurements to suit your frame (this would be an appropriate size for frame A). Hinge the two pieces together at the top with a piece of thin card as indicated in the diagram, folded in half as the broken line. Fix ribbon through the two holes, adjusting the length so that the picture stands at the required angle when the thin strut is glued to the back of the frame.

Key to frames overleaf
A　Tiny yellow stylised flowers on a grey ground, narrowly edged with black, make a smart frame that would 'fit in' almost anywhere – or make an ideal gift for a man. The black braid round the outside is cut in half to edge the inner circle.
B　A very masculine frame, smoothly covered with fine cord. The soft olive colour is tastefully set off by a slightly smaller inner mount cut from stiff paper in a toning shade of brown.
C　So clean and simple – another design that would be 'right' almost anywhere. The coffee-coloured fabric with a stylised pattern in white happens to be cotton sheeting. The effect is so smart that no other trim is needed.
D　Pure Victoriana in a double frame of linked circles covered with a miniature rose print. Narrow lampshade braid echoes the green leaves – and the butterfly bow (see Finishing Touches) emphasises the romance of this nostalgic design. (Points B are 3.5cm (13/8in) from A on a 13cm (5in) length of 9mm (3/8in) wide single-face satin ribbon.)

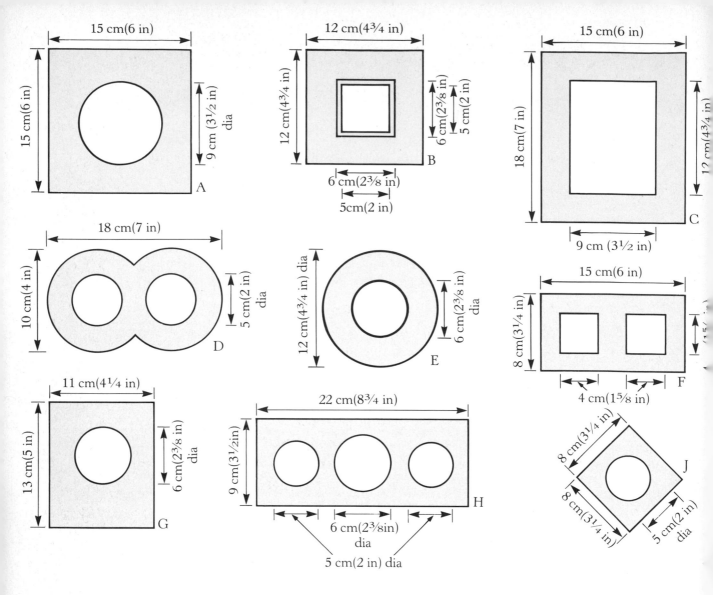

E *Very* unsophisticated, this one! Young and feminine – perfect for a pretty bedroom. The mount is covered with fresh pink and white check gingham, with pink lace tightly stretched over the outer edge. The inner edge is decorated with an embroidered flower trim – and three deep pink satin roses add the crowning touch. Ribbon roses are on page 9; the central one is made from 20cm (8in) of 9mm (⅜in) wide ribbon, and the smaller ones from 15cm (6in) of 6mm (¼in) wide ribbon.

F Another very versatile design. Two square pictures in a double frame severely covered in plain dark green cotton, which dramatically sets off the very narrow gold filigree braid border.

G An azure blue fabric printed with tiny white flowers, edged with scalloped lace. Be sparing with the glue – just dab it behind the densest part of the lace to hold it in position on the right side; take the straight edge over to the back. Tiny pale blue pearls circle the centre; buy them by the metre/yard, firmly fixed to the string to avoid accidents. A narrow trail of glue will hold them in place.

H A busy pattern of tiny flowers and leaves in two shades of blue is ideal for this triple frame. Narrow toning blue lampshade braid is glued flat around the outer edge, just slightly overlapping.

J Lilac voile with a flock spot (dotted Swiss) for a demure little diamond-shaped hanging frame. Shimmering pearl beads circle the centre: and a very narrow guipure lace creates the frosty edge (see frame G for notes on fixing the pearls and lace). A dainty satin butterfly bow (see Finishing Touches) adds the final touch to this charming design; points B are 2.5cm (1in) from A on a 10cm (4in) length of 9mm (⅜in) wide single-face satin ribbon.

The Bears' Story

PART THREE

Apple Bear pinned a satin rose onto a tiny hat and studied it critically. Apple Bear was determined to win the prize for the Best Christmas Stocking of All.

Every Christmas Eve, on the stroke of midnight, each bear packed all his gifts into a Christmas stocking. Then Santa went through them, unpacking each one and examining the contents in great detail. And the bear whose work was judged the best had the wonderful thrill of being allowed to ride on Santa's sleigh and help him deliver the stockings.

As he peered furtively round at the other bears' gifts, Apple Bear suddenly noticed a trail of fine thread across the floor. 'Hi!' he shouted, grabbing at it.

The other bears all looked up in surprise.

'It's that thieving Christmas Mouse again,' he cried, as something disappeared through a hole in the skirting board. 'It's just stolen my reel of thread.'

APPLE BEAR'S
Christmas Stocking Gifts

Little things, sweetly scented, unashamedly feminine, designed to captivate the woman with romance in her heart, be she nine years old or ninety. The materials cost little or nothing, but the loving care you put into making them will be reflected in such pretty details as tiny satin roses, woven ribbons and enchanting confections of miniature millinery.

FIVE LITTLE LAVENDER MAIDS

Five little ladies to fire your imagination. The basic design couldn't be more simple; a narrow bag made from satin ribbon, filled with dried lavender flowers, and topped with a craft ball. Add some embroidery wool hair . . . then let fashion go to your head, and become your very own costume designer. The result is the daintiest bit of frippery imaginable to adorn a feminine dressing table.

Try to keep to one colour scheme for each doll; sort through your hoarded leftovers for tiny bits and pieces of felt, ribbon, lace, braid, beads, flowers, feathers and so on, choosing colours which either match or tone with the satin ribbon you have used for the body. Have them all laid out on your work-table – then let the materials you have available suggest the design of your

costume. Make a rough pencil sketch of your planned doll, jotting down notes and ideas and different alternatives to consider at a later stage, as the design develops. You can see the effect of this kind of careful preliminary planning when you study the photograph.

Following the directions for the basic figure, precise details are given for each of the five maids illustrated in the photograph. Your own little maids will, of course, be determined by what you find in your personal piece bag. Nevertheless, if you want to follow a specific feature from an individual doll, like a cape, a hat or a hemline, you should find the patterns, methods and measurements a helpful guide.

The Basic Figure

MATERIALS

20cm (8in) single-face satin ribbon, 39mm (1½in) wide
15cm (6in) satin ribbon, 1.5mm (¹⁄₁₆in) wide, to hang
Flesh-tinted turned paper craft ball, 3cm (1¼in) diameter
8cm (3in) pipe cleaner (chenille stem)
Seven 76cm (30in) strands Twilley's stranded embroidery wool, or fine knitting yarn, for hair
Polyester filling (or cotton wool)
Flesh-coloured poster paint (if ball is not coloured)
Black or dark brown/sepia ball-point pen, pencil or ink
Stiff card
Tiny pin (optional)
Dried lavender
Clear adhesive

Figure 1

1 Tack 5mm (¼in) under at each end of the wide ribbon. Fold the ribbon in half, right side inside as figure 1, and oversew the woven edges together to form a 'bag' (make tiny stitches, catching just the very edge of the ribbon).

2 Gather round the top, close to the folded edge, but don't draw up.

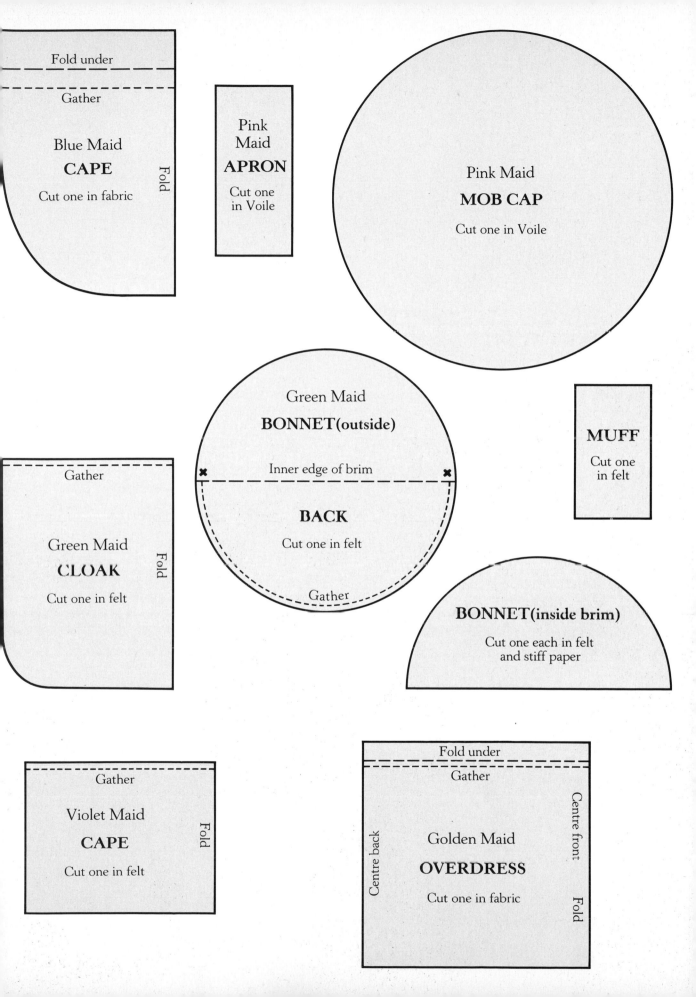

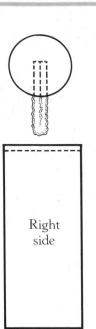

Right
side

Figure 2

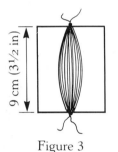

9 cm (3½ in)

Figure 3

Figure 4

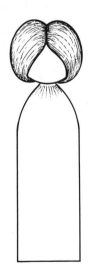

Figure 5

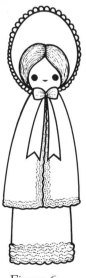

Figure 6

3 Turn to the right side and three-quarters fill with lavender (using a funnel), then lightly fill the top of the bag with stuffing or cotton wool.

4 Bend the pipe cleaner in half and push the ends firmly up into the ball (figure 2). Then lower the bent end into the top of the bag and draw up the gathers tightly, catching the pipe cleaner securely into place.

5 Put six strands of embroidery wool together and wind them smoothly and evenly round a 9cm (3in) deep piece of card. Tie the resulting skein tightly at each edge with a single strand of wool (figure 3). Then slip the skein off the card and tie it *loosely* at the centre (figure 4). Glue the loosely tied centre of the skein to the top of the head, then glue each side of the skein to the side of the head, joining the two tied ends at the nape of the neck, centre back of head (figure 5). Stitch the back with a single strand, drawing the front hair neatly round and catching the sides of the skein together to cover the back of the head. Trim off any untidy ends.

6 You can, if you wish, mark the features now, but it is usually better to wait until the doll is finished (figure 6). Draw round dots for the eyes (indicate them first in pencil) and make a tiny straight line between them, for the nose, level with the bottom of the eyes (the nose may be omitted, if preferred).

7 When the doll is complete, stitch or pin the ends of the narrow ribbon to the top of the head, forming a loop to hang.

The Blue Maid

A band of 10mm (⅜in) deep white lace is stitched around the bag so that it overlaps the bottom; then another row is sewn around the hemline of the dress, so that it overlaps the top edge of the first row. It is finished with a band of narrow (about 7-8mm [¼in]) blue braid glued over the top edge of the second row of lace.

The cape (see pattern) is cut in a light-to-medium-weight printed cotton-type fabric (cut along the thread and draw a few threads, to prevent fraying). Turn the top edge under along the broken line, then gather 5mm (¼in) below the fold to form a collar – but don't draw up yet. Trim the raw edge with very narrow lace or braid (the cape illustrated is trimmed with the same braid used for the hem, cut along the centre to make it half the width). Draw up the gathers tightly around the neck, and secure.

A few tiny flowers are bound together with thread to form a posy, then stitched to the front of the dress between the edges of the cape. A short length of 3mm (⅛in) wide satin ribbon is tied around the back of the posy, to hang down below.

The hat is 25cm (10in) of blue-and-white lace, 10mm (⅜in) deep, with the cut ends glued together to form a circle; then the straight edge is gathered and drawn up to form a rosette with a hole about 1cm (⅜in) in the centre. A 10cm (4in) length of blue feather-edge 5mm (¼in) wide satin ribbon is folded in half, and the fold pinned to the top of the head so that the ends hang down at the back to form ties; then the rosette is glued to the top of the head. The crowning glory is a blue satin rose (see page 9) made from 25cm (10in) of 10mm (⅜in) wide ribbon, glued in the centre.

Tiny pearl bead earrings are glued at each side of the face.

The Pink Maid

Two layers of 15mm (⅝in) deep cream lace are stitched around the bottom of the bag, just as for the Blue Maid, then a very narrow band of wine-coloured braid is glued just below the top edge of the second row of lace.

A 15cm (6in) length of the same lace is gathered around the neck to form her collar, joined at the back.

Her apron (see pattern) is cut in cream voile (cut along the thread of the fabric, to prevent fraying). The top edge is glued behind the centre of a 10cm (4in) length of 3mm (⅛in) wide wine satin ribbon. Then the ribbon is glued around the body, about 1.5cm (⅝in) below the collar.

The mob cap (see pattern) is also cut in cream voile. Turn under and stitch a very narrow hem around the edge of the circle. Then, with a gathering stitch, sew the top edge of some 10mm (⅜in) deep lace close to the edge, so that most of it overlaps (the lace won't be flat; don't worry). Draw up and fit on the head, pulling most of gathers around to the sides and front before catching the cap securely into position. The tiny bow glued at the centre front above the lace frill is the same ribbon used for the waistband.

The Green Maid

The band of 10mm (⅜in) wide green braid glued around the bottom of the bag has heavy cream lace, about 7-8mm (¼in) deep, immediately above it.

Her cloak (see pattern) is cut in green felt and edged with narrow (about 7-8mm [¼in] wide) green braid. Gather very close to the top edge and draw up tightly around the neck, joining the top corners at the centre front.

Cut the outside and inside brim of the bonnet (see patterns) in felt; then cut the inner brim again in stiff paper. Glue the paper over one half of the circle of felt (on the wrong side), then glue the semi-circle of felt on top. Glue cream lace (as above) around the inside brim, just overlapping the edge. Fit the bonnet on the doll, pinning the corners of the brim (points marked x) to each side of the head, then gather round the curved lower edge at the back and draw up to fit. Catch the bonnet securely to the head.

The bonnet and muff are trimmed with green-and-cream plaited braid. To make this, fold a 70cm (¾yd) length of 1.5mm (¹⁄₁₆in) wide satin ribbon in half, and glue one end of a 35cm (⅜yd) length of cream ribbon inside the fold; plait neatly as directed on page 8. Glue this braid all round the outer edge of the bonnet.

The bonnet is completed with a 15cm (6in) length of 6mm (¼in) wide green satin ribbon, the centre gathered and fixed under the chin, then the ends taken up over the bonnet and joined on top. Two small fluffy feathers are trimmed to shape and glued over the top of the bonnet brim. The butterfly bow (see Finishing Touches) glued under her chin is made from 8cm (3¼in) of the same green ribbon; points B are 2cm (¾in) from A.

Cut the muff in felt (see pattern), then roll it round and join the short edges. Glue plaited braid around each end. Glue (or stitch) to the front of the figure, over front edges of cloak.

The Violet Maid

The hem of the dress is two rows of 10mm (⅜in) deep black lace, exactly as described for the Blue Maid. A row of 10mm (⅜in) wide guipure lace daisies, in the same colour as the dress, is glued down the centre front.

Her cape (see pattern) is cut in violet felt. The lower edge is trimmed with the same black lace as the hem, and this lace is also sewn along the top edge with a

gathering stitch, so that it forms a frilled stand-up collar when the gathers are drawn up tightly around her neck; but before doing this, trim the front edges with the very narrowest black braid.

Her boater is made from black raffia (natural raffia may be coloured with a permanent black felt marker, or painted with black ink, when the hat is finished). Make a knot at one end of the raffia, then wind the raffia around the knot, keeping it absolutely flat, and stitching it into place with matching thread (see figure 7). Continue in this way, taking care to keep the work absolutely flat, until you have a circle 2.5cm (1in) in diameter. Then turn and stitch the next round at right angles to the edge of the circle, to form the sides of the hat. Continue in this direction for 8-10mm (¼-⅜in), then turn outwards to make the brim, finishing off the edge neatly when the hat is about 4cm (1½-1⅝in) in diameter.

Figure 7

A band of 3mm (⅛in) wide satin ribbon trims the boater, with a butterfly bow (see Finishing Touches) at the back made from 8cm (3¼in) of 9mm (⅜in) wide satin ribbon in the same shade; points B are 2.5cm (1in) from A. A lilac rose (see Finishing Touches) is glued at the centre front, made from 15cm (6in) of 6mm (¼in) wide satin ribbon.

Her earrings are tiny dark purple beads glued at each side of her face.

The Golden Maid

A double layer of 2.5cm (1in) deep silky dark brown lampshade fringe hangs down below the bottom of the bag, then 15cm (6in) of yellow lace, 15mm (⅝in) deep, is gathered over the top edge of the fringe.

Her overdress (see pattern) is cut in yellow spotted voile. Join the centre back seam and turn to the right side. The same yellow lace is stitched around the lower edge, with a row of embroidered trimming on top and down the centre front. Turn the raw top edge under and stitch yellow lace level with the fold, using a gathering stitch. Fit the overdress on the doll and draw up round the neck so that the lace forms a collar. A tiny rose made from 3mm (⅛in) wide ribbon decorates the collar.

Her hat is made from dark brown raffia, working a flat circle exactly as described for the crown of the Violet Maid's boater — but continuing until it is 5cm (2in) in diameter. The cut ends of a 15cm (6in) length of the same yellow lace are glued together, and then the straight edge gathered and drawn up to form a rosette with a 1cm (⅜in) hole in the centre. This is stitched centrally on top of the hat. Immediately behind the lace is a butterfly bow (see Finishing Touches) made from 15cm (6in) of deep gold satin ribbon, 12mm (½in) wide (points B are 4.5cm [1¾in] from A). A few pale and deep yellow forget-me-nots are stitched on top of the lace, heads all facing forward. Finally, three roses are glued on top, each made from 15cm (6in) sable brown satin ribbon, 6mm (¼in) wide. The hat can be either stitched or glued to the top of the head, tilted well forward.

The tiniest pearl beads make her earrings.

NINE POT-POURRI SACHETS

The heady scent of pot-pourri evokes all the warmth and sunshine of a summer garden. Great-grandmama would have stitched it into tiny sachets, just like these, for her own drawers and dressing table or for her friends. So why not do the same, and give yourself a double dose of nostalgia?

But if Great-grandmama is looking in, she'll envy you all the advantages of modern methods and materials. No hassle making your own pot-pourri any more, if you don't want to; there's a wide variety available in the shops these days. Choose a fine one, without any large pieces -- and if necessary, crush it with a pestle and mortar. And the sachets themselves, which are made from odd scraps of fabric left over from previous projects, are trimmed with non-iron lace and ribbons.

MATERIALS

Two pieces of lightweight firmly woven cotton-type fabric,
  a little larger than the pattern
Lace or broderie anglaise (eyelet embroidery) edging (see
  individual sachet notes below)
Ribbons to trim (see individual sachet notes below)
Embroidered motifs, narrow braid, etc, to trim (see
  individual sachet notes below)
Matching threads
Pot-pourri to fill
Clear adhesive

1 Trace your chosen shape. Place the two pieces of fabric right sides together, and pin the pattern on top. Stitch neatly round, close to the edge of the pattern, leaving open between the notches.

2 Cut around the stitched shape (with pinking shears if possible) leaving a very narrow seam, then remove the pattern. Turn back the raw edge at each side of the opening and tack, then turn to the right side.

3 Fill with pot-pourri, and oversew (overcast) the edges neatly together.

4 Stitch lace or broderie anglaise (eyelet embroidery) all round the edge of the sachet, keeping it flat on straight edges, gathering generously on corners, but gathering only just enough around curves without forming a frill (unless using pre-filled lace).

5 Decorate the sachet to your own design, or make trimmings as described below (see Finishing Touches for full instructions) and glue or stitch securely into place.

Simply Square Sachet

Blue gingham – very easy, but very effective. Edged with blue-and-white lace (30cm [12in] x 10mm [3⁄8in] deep); then a bow at each corner and a purchased flower motif embroidery in the centre. Butterfly bows are 8cm (3in) single-face satin ribbon, 6mm (1⁄4in) wide; points B are 2cm (3⁄8in) from A.

Forget-me-not print – another very simple idea – and even quicker to do. The edging is scalloped white lace (30cm [12in] x 10mm [3⁄8in] deep). And a 13cm (5in) length of miniature white guipure lace hearts forms a circle on a dark blue ground patterned with tiny forget-me-nots.

Olive green cotton – a little more work in this one. The cream cotton lace is much heavier, and a little narrower (30cm (12in) x 7-8mm [1⁄4in] deep). A creamy coffee border of satin ribbon set against it, tones with the cream, lemon and peach rosebuds nestling amongst fresh green leaves.

Make the plaited braid (see Finishing Touches) from three 50cm (20in) lengths of 1.5mm (1⁄16in) ribbon, and glue the extra piece at the end round to form a loop. Each rosebud is 15cm (6in) single-face satin ribbon, 6mm (1⁄4in) wide. And you'll need 15cm (6in) single-face ribbon, 15mm (5⁄8in) wide, for the leaves; each one is a 5cm (1in) length, folded in half.

White spotted voile (dotted Swiss) – white scalloped lace (30cm [12in] x 10mm [3⁄8in] deep) bordering latticed and plaited satin ribbons, with a miniature rose in the centre. This design has a particularly Victorian air, which is emphasised by the delicate iris and light orchid colour combination. Criss-cross 3mm (1⁄8in) wide satin ribbon from corner to corner, then cross these with shorter pieces meeting at the centre of each side, as illustrated (40cm [1⁄2in] ribbon in all). Plait three 40cm (16in) lengths of 1.5mm (1⁄16in) wide ribbon (see Finishing Touches) and glue round the edge, over the cut ends. Make the miniature rose from 10cm (4in) satin ribbon, 3mm (1⁄8in) wide.

Round and Rosy Sachet

Pale lilac print – 30cm (12in) matching lace, 12mm (1⁄2in) deep, edges this one. Another 15cm (6in) is gathered to make the central rosette; leave a tiny hole in which to set the rose, which is made from 15cm (6in) single-face satin ribbon, 6mm (1⁄4in) wide. The rose picks up the middle one of the three 'African violet' shades that make the plaited border (30cm [12in] x 1.5mm [1⁄16in] wide of each).

Yellow spotted voile (dotted Swiss) – a slightly wider pale coffee lace echoes the soft sable brown plaited border and central rose, set on a dramatic deep yellow satin bow. You will need 30cm (12in) lace, 15mm (5⁄8in) deep; 90cm (1yd) satin ribbon, 1.5mm (1⁄16in) wide, for the plaited edge (see Finishing Touches); 25cm (10in) single-face satin ribbon, 6mm (1⁄4in) wide, for the rose; and 13cm (5in) single-face satin, 15mm (5⁄8in) wide, for the butterfly bow (page 9: points B are 3.5cm [13⁄8in] from A).

Pink-and-white print – pink and white lace (30cm

SIMPLY

SQUARE

Leave open

HEARTS AND

FLOWERS

Leave open

ROUND AND

ROSY

Leave open

NINE POT-POURRI SACHETS:

[12in] x 10mm [³⁄₈in] deep) matches the delicate fabric. Then one 30cm (12in) length of 1.5mm (¹⁄₁₆in) wide deep pink ribbon is plaited with two of silver satin for the border (see Finishing Touches). The deep pink rose in the centre is 15cm (6in) of 6mm (¹⁄₄in) wide single-face satin, and its three shimmering silver leaves are each cut from a 2.5cm (1in) length of 15mm (⁵⁄₈in) wide silver metallic grosgrain ribbon.

Hearts and Flowers Sachet

Rosebud print – white scalloped lace (30cm [12in] x 10mm [³⁄₈in] deep) is traditionally romantic around this pretty sachet. The dark green leaves of the rosebud printed cotton are matched with a 6-7mm (¹⁄₄in) wide silky lampshade braid, cut down the centre to make it even narrower (12.5cm [5in] = 25cm [10in] half-width). And the deep rose of the printed flowers is echoed in a big satin butterfly bow (see Finishing Touches) made from 13cm (5in) single-face satin ribbon, 12mm (¹⁄₂in) wide: points B are 3.5cm (1³⁄₈in) from A.

Cream spotted voile (dotted Swiss) – matching cream pre-frilled lace (25cm [10in] x 10mm [³⁄₈in] deep) is easy to apply. And the heart shape is emphasised with plaited braid (see Finishing Touches) in a soft willow green (plait three 30cm [12in] lengths of 1.5mm [¹⁄₁₆in] wide ribbon). Another three 8cm (3in) lengths of the ribbon form streamers at the centre of the heart, and the three gauzy fabric leaves are cut down from larger purchased ones. The full-blown heliotrope rose is 25cm (10in) single-face 6mm (¹⁄₄in) wide ribbon.

THREE OLD-FASHIONED LAVENDER FAGGOTS

A tiny basket of satin ribbon cages the lavender flowers in this charming reminder of a cottage craft from centuries past. In country districts these dainty little batons were traditionally woven as a betrothal gift for a bride-to-be by her girl-friends.

This is especially for those well-organised people who plan ahead for Christmas. The first stage has to be done in the summer, when the fresh lavender is coming into flower and the stalks are strong and supple. But you can leave the finishing off and fancy trimmings until nearer Christmas, if you wish.

With their romantic history, lavender faggots make an unusual and attractive stocking-filler. But they have a practical purpose too; when the young bride became a housewife, she placed them between the folded sheets and pillowcases in her linen closet, not only to make everything fresh and fragrant – but to keep the moths away as well.

MATERIALS

Fresh lavender (about eleven firm, strong stalks)
2m (2yd) satin ribbon, 3mm (⅛in) wide
30cm (12in) satin ribbon, 1.5mm (1/16in) wide, for the loop
15cm (6in) single-face satin ribbon, 6mm (¼in) wide, for the rose
25cm (10in) feather-edge satin ribbon, 5mm (¼in) wide, for the bow
10cm (4in) narrow lace, about 10mm (⅜in) wide
Matching threads
Clear adhesive

1 Pick the lavender when the stalks are fresh and green and supple, and the flowers are just coming out. You must have an odd number of stalks – eleven is often a good number to work with. Bunch them tightly and neatly together; for instance, if you are working with eleven stalks, have five heads around one central one which stands half-a-head above the others. Then arrange the remaining five heads around the previous ones, half-a-head lower than the first five.

2 Tie one end of the 3mm (⅛in) wide ribbon tightly around the stalks, immediately below the flower heads. Then one-by-one, and very carefully, bend the stalks back over the flower heads. When the heads are surrounded by the stalks, turn the whole thing round so that the stalks are hanging down again, and begin to weave the ribbon in and out between them. Keep the ribbon smooth and even and taut.

Continue weaving until the flowers are completely encased: then stop, without cutting the ribbon or finishing off. Leave in a dry, sunny place for about a week, until the lavender has dried and shrunk – and the ribbon has become loose.

3 Beginning at the top, use the points of your small scissors or a fine knitting needle or skewer to draw out and pull up the slack ribbon, making it taut again; work round and round, until you reach the bottom. Bind the ribbon round the stalks twice, then cut and glue the end.

4 Cut the stalks, leaving enough to form the handle of the baton. The total length will depend on the depth of the woven area, but if this measures about 8cm (3in), 20cm (8in) is a good overall measurement for the faggot.

5 Fold the very narrow ribbon in half and knot it to form a loop 7cm (2¾in) long. Bind the two ends twice around the stalks, about 3cm (1¼in) from the bottom, and then knot them tightly, 'losing' the ends by pushing them between the stalks of the handle.

6 Make the feather-edge ribbon into a butterfly bow (see Finishing Touches), but don't gather it; mark points B 6cm (2⅜in) from A as directed, but take your needle through the *centre* of the ribbon at these points, then arrange the loops attractively before taking two or three stitches through the ribbon to hold the shape of the bow. Stitch to the faggot, immediately below the woven section.

7 Glue the cut ends of the lace together, then gather the straight edge and draw up to form a rosette with a 5mm (¼in) diameter hole in the centre. Glue it over the centre of the bow.

8 Make a ribbon rose as directed on page 9 and glue it in the centre of the lace.

The Bears' Story

PART FOUR

Damson Bear embroidered a neat black line around a bright-green caterpillar on an orange pencil case. Then he set it down beside four other pencil cases. On the other side of the table lay six purses with animal faces.

A shadow fell across his work, and Damson Bear looked up to see Santa Claus standing behind him.

'You've done very well this year,' Santa smiled approvingly. 'Your stitching has improved, and I like the colours you have chosen.'

Damson Bear glowed with pride.

'I'm going to feed the reindeer,' Santa told him, buttoning up his check shirt. 'Will you make me a corned-beef sandwich while I'm outside?'

Damson Bear hurried over to the kitchen corner to make the sandwich. He wanted to be sure it was specially delicious, to keep in Santa's good books.

But whilst he was decorating it with a sprig of watercress . . . the Christmas Mouse scampered in and stole his best pair of scissors.

DAMSON BEAR'S
Christmas Stocking Gifts

Practical things, but fun too. Leftover pieces of fur fabric make endearing animal purses; there's a puppy, a kitten, a bunny, a bear (of course), a lion or an owl to choose from. And useful pencil cases in bright colours, with amusing decoration to make boring homework a bit more bearable.

SIX POCKET MONEY PETS

Quick to make and quick to please . . . they'll be quick to sell, too – if you've profit as well as pocket money in mind for these amusing purses. Just the right size for a child's hands, with a zip and a strap to ensure that small owners are not parted from their property.

Note: work with right sides together unless otherwise instructed; oversew (overcast) all seams.

Arrows indicate direction of pile when cutting out fur; stroke it to find the *smooth* way.

Puppy

MATERIALS

Cream fur fabric, 15cm (6in) deep x 35cm (14in) wide
Brown fur fabric, 15cm (6in) deep x 35cm (14in) wide
5cm (2in) square of black felt (or scraps) for features
15cm (6in) zip fastener
1m (1yd) narrow braid or lacing cord
Matching threads

1 Cut the head once, and the ear twice (reversing the second piece) in each colour fur (note direction of arrows).

2 Right sides facing, oversew (overcast) the two head pieces together, leaving open across the top between the notches. Turn under and tack a very narrow hem along both these raw edges. Turn to the right side.

3 Fit the zip across the top and stitch it securely into place (don't have the fur too close to the teeth, to avoid it catching when in use; if necessary, trim the fur slightly to clear the opening).

4 Right sides together, join a brown and a cream ear all round, leaving open between the top point and the notch. Turn under and tack a very narrow hem along both raw edges, then turn to the right side and slipstitch the edges together. Prepare the second ear in the same way.

5 Pin the ears to the cream head, positioning them as illustrated.

6 Cut the eyes and nose in felt. Pin them to the face (be guided by the pattern, but check to your own satisfaction that they are in the best position); when you are happy, appliqué them into place.

7 Cut the braid or cord to the required length for the strap, and stitch the ends securely at each end of the zip.

Bear

MATERIALS

Camel fur, 15cm (6in) deep x 50cm (20in) wide
5 x 6cm (2 x 2½in) camel felt for the face
5cm (2in) square of black felt (or scraps) for features
15cm (6in) zip fastener
1m (1yd) narrow braid or lacing cord
Black stranded embroidery cotton (floss)
Matching threads

1 Cut the head twice, and the ear four times, in fur fabric (note direction of arrows). Cut the face once in camel felt.

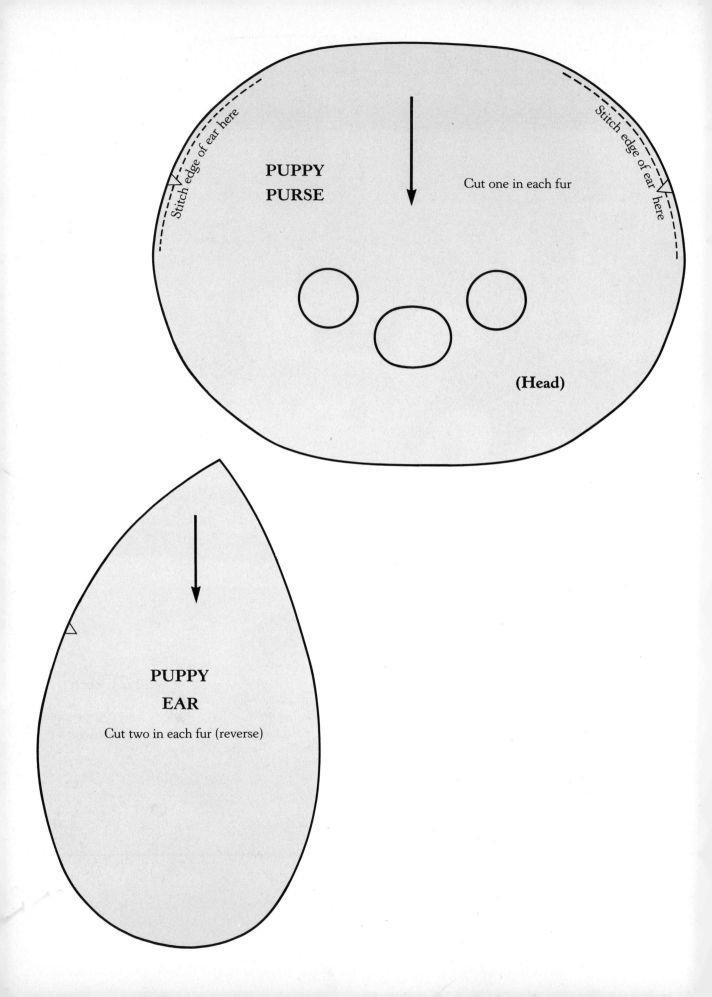

PUPPY
PURSE

Cut one in each fur

Stitch edge of ear here

Stitch edge of ear here

(Head)

PUPPY
EAR

Cut two in each fur (reverse)

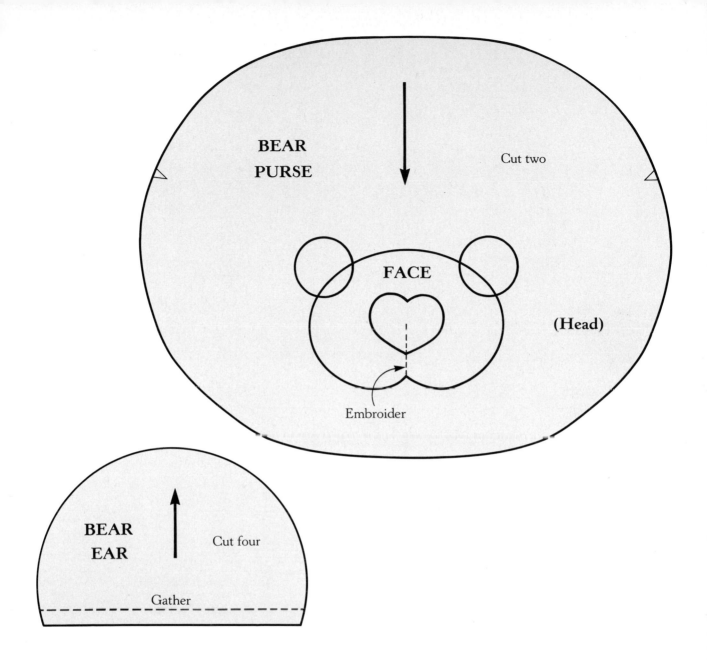

BEAR PURSE

Cut two

FACE

(Head)

Embroider

BEAR EAR

Cut four

Gather

2 Right sides facing, oversew (overcast) the two head pieces together, leaving open across the top between the notches. Turn under and tack a very narrow hem along both these raw edges. Turn to the right side.

3 Fit the zip across the top and stitch it securely into place (don't have the fur too close to the teeth, to avoid it catching when in use; if necessary, trim the fur slightly to clear the opening).

4 To make each ear, join two pieces all round, leaving the straight lower edge open; turn to the right side. Gather the two pieces together along the lower edge and draw up tightly to measure 2cm (¾in). Pin to the

front head as illustrated, but don't stitch into place yet.

5 Cut the eyes and nose in black felt. Embroider the black line on the face in stem (outline) stitch, using three strands of embroidery cotton. Then appliqué the nose on top, as indicated. Pin the face to the front head, positioned as indicated on the pattern, then appliqué. Finally, appliqué the eyes into place.

Adjust the position of the ears, if necessary, then stitch securely.

6 Cut the braid or cord to the required length for the strap, and stitch the ends securely at each end of the zip.

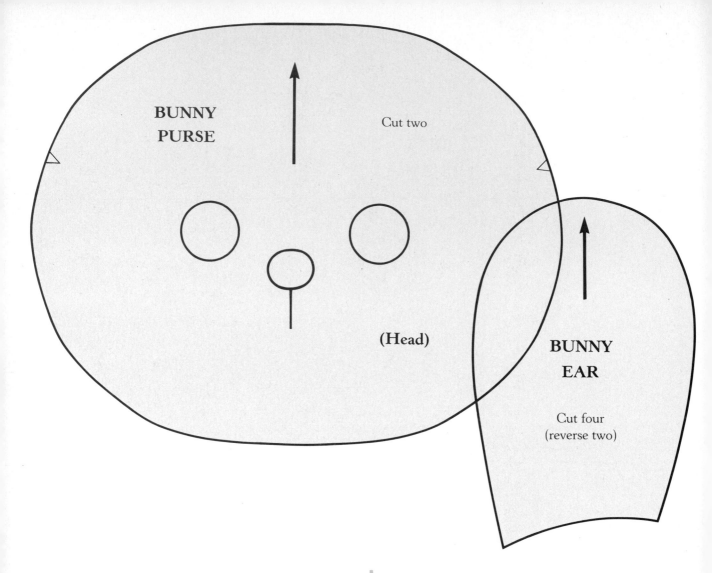

BUNNY PURSE

Cut two

(Head)

BUNNY EAR

Cut four
(reverse two)

Bunny

MATERIALS

Light-grey fur fabric, 15cm (6in) deep x 60cm (24in) wide
5cm (2in) square of black felt (or scraps) for features
15cm (6in) zip fastener
1m (1yd) narrow braid or lacing cord
Black stranded embroidery cotton (floss)
Matching threads

1 Cut the head twice, and the ear four times (reversing two), in fur fabric (note direction of arrows).

2 Right sides facing, oversew (overcast) the two head pieces together, leaving open across the top between the notches. Turn under and tack a very narrow hem along both these raw edges. Turn to the right side.

3 Fit the zip across the top and stitch it securely into place (don't have the fur too close to the teeth, to avoid it catching when in use; if necessary, trim the fur slightly to clear the opening).

4 To make each ear, join two pieces all round, leaving the straight lower edge open; turn to the right side. Pin to the *back* head as illustrated, then stitch securely.

5 Using six strands of embroidery cotton (floss), make one or two straight stitches in the centre of the face, as indicated on the pattern.

6 Cut the eyes and nose in black felt. Appliqué the nose over the top of the embroidered line, as shown. Finally pin, then appliqué, the eyes into position.

7 Cut the braid or cord to the required length for the strap, and stitch the ends securely to the tips of the ears.

Owl

MATERIALS

Dark-brown fur fabric, 15cm (6in) deep x 45cm (18in) wide
4 x 10cm (1½ x 4in) beige felt, for eyelids
7 x 10cm (2½ x 4in) lemon-yellow felt, for outer eyes
4 x 8cm (1½ x 3in) golden-brown felt, for inner eyes
5cm (2in) square of black felt (or scraps), for pupils
4 x 8cm (1½ x 3in) orange felt, for beak
40cm (15in) very narrow cream braid (if possible, cut
    narrow braid down centre – or use plaited ribbon [page 8]
2 black sequins, about 8mm (5/16in) diameter (optional)
Tiny scrap of stuffing (or cotton wool)
15cm (6in) zip fastener
1m (1yd) narrow braid or lacing cord
Matching threads
Clear adhesive (optional)

1 Cut the head twice, and the ear four times, in fur fabric (note direction of arrows).

2 Right sides facing, oversew (overcast) the two head pieces together, leaving open across the top between the notches. Turn under and tack a very narrow hem along both these raw edges. Turn to the right side.

3 Fit the zip across the top and stitch it securely into place (don't have the fur too close to the teeth, to avoid it catching when in use; if necessary, trim the fur slightly to clear the opening).

4 To make each ear, join two pieces all round, leaving the straight lower edge open; turn to the right side. Gather the two pieces together along the lower edge, and draw up to measure about 3cm (1¼in); then fold the ear in half as the broken line and catch together.

5 Pin the ears, then stitch them very securely, close to the top of the front head, as illustrated.

6 Cut the outer eye twice in yellow felt, the inner eye twice in golden-brown, the pupil twice in black, and the eyelid twice in beige.
  To prepare each eye, glue (or appliqué) the pupil in the centre of the inner eye, then stitch a sequin on top. Following the pattern for guidance, glue (or appliqué) the golden-brown eye to the yellow outer eye. Glue (or appliqué) the eyelid on top, as indicated. Glue (or stitch) very narrow braid all round the edge.

7 Cut the beak twice in orange felt and oversew (over-cast) together round the two sides, leaving open across the top. Push a tiny bit of stuffing inside, then oversew (overcast) across the top.

8 Pin the eyes to the head, positioned as the pattern, and check that the beak sits nicely in the position indicated. Stitch the eyes into place (*don't* appliqué; stitch just inside the braid). Then stitch the beak into place across the top, leaving the beak itself free.

9 Cut the braid or cord to the required length for the strap, and stitch the ends securely at each end of the zip.

Kitten

MATERIALS

Dark-grey fur fabric, 15cm (6in) deep x 40cm (15in) wide
3 x 4cm (1¼ x 1½in) pink felt for the nose
4 x 8cm (1½ x 3in) light olive green felt for the eyes
2.5 x 5cm (1 x 2in) black felt (or scraps) for the pupils
2 silver sequins, about 8mm (5/16in) diameter
15cm (6in) zip fastener
1m (1yd) narrow braid or lacing cord
Matching threads

1 Cut the head twice in fur fabric. Cut the nose once, and the eye and pupil twice each, in the appropriate felts (reverse the second eye).

2 Right sides facing, oversew (overcast) the two pieces together, leaving open across the top between the tips of the ears.

3 Fit the zip across the top and stitch it securely into place, easing the fur fabric in to fit the zip (don't have the fur too close to the teeth; if necessary, trim the fur slightly to clear the opening).

4 Appliqué the pupils to the eyes, following the pattern. Then cut a fraction off the base of each sequin, and stitch them in the centre of the pupils, the straight cut edge of the sequin level with the straight edge of the pupil.

5 Pin the nose into position in the centre of the face, following the pattern. Then pin the eyes into position and appliqué them all into place.

6 Cut the braid or cord to the required length for the strap, and stitch the ends securely to the tips of the ears.

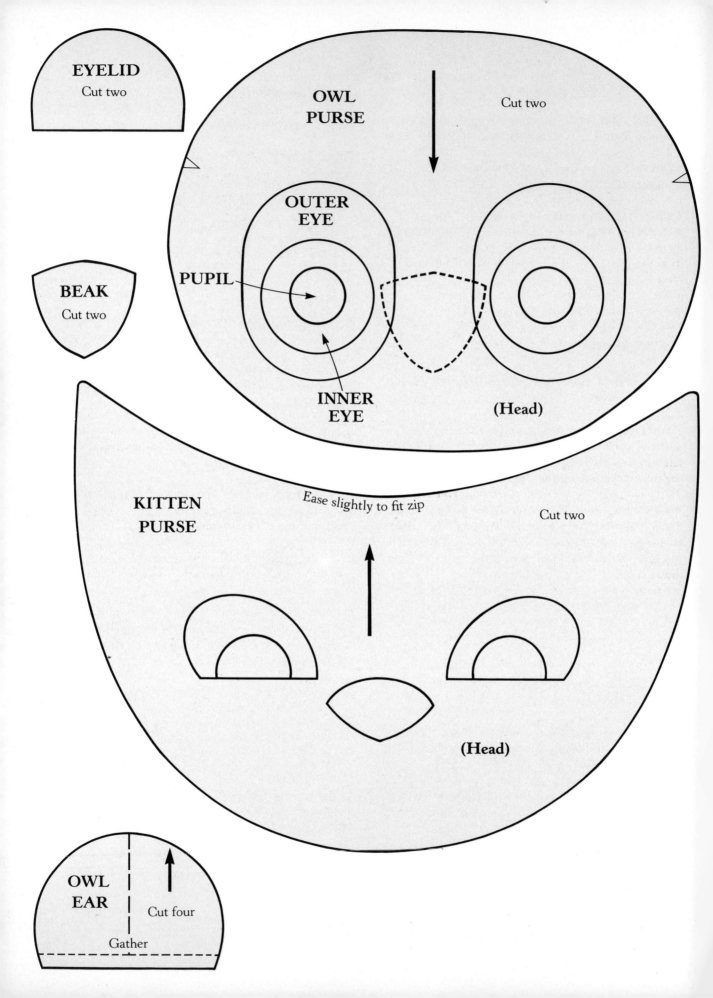

EYELID
Cut two

OWL PURSE
Cut two

OUTER EYE

PUPIL

BEAK
Cut two

INNER EYE

(Head)

Ease slightly to fit zip

KITTEN PURSE

Cut two

(Head)

OWL EAR
Cut four

Gather

Lion

MATERIALS

Shaggy golden-brown fur fabric, 3cm (1¼in) deep x 50cm (20in) wide

15 x 40cm (6 x 16in) golden-brown felt *or* a 25cm (10in) square

2.5 x 6cm (1 x 2½in) mid-brown felt, for inner eyes

4 x 7cm (1½ x 2¾in) white felt, for outer eyes

5cm (2in) square of black felt (or scraps), for nose and pupils

3 x 2cm (1¼ x ¾in) pink felt, for tongue

2 black sequins, about 8mm (⁵⁄₁₆in) diameter (optional)

15cm (6in) zip fastener

1m (1yd) narrow braid or lacing cord

Black stranded embroidery cotton (floss)

Matching threads

Clear adhesive (optional)

1 Cut the head twice, and the face once, in golden-brown felt.

2 Pin the strip of fur fabric to one of the head pieces, with the wrong side of the fur to the right side of the felt and the outer edges of the fur and felt level; have the pile of the fur directed *outwards* beyond the edge of the felt (as arrows). Oversew (overcast) the edges of the fur fabric and felt together; when you have sewn the fur strip all the way round, trim off the excess, allowing a small overlap. Stitch the join neatly.

Gather around the inner edge of the fur strip. Then draw up the gathers so that the fur lies flat on the felt; catch the fur lightly to the felt to hold it in place.

3 Cut the outer eye twice in white felt, the inner eye in brown and the pupils and nose in black. Cut the tongue in pink felt.

4 Using three strands of embroidery cotton (floss), embroider the short line on the face below the nose, in stem (outline) stitch, as indicated on the pattern. Then glue (or appliqué) the nose over the top of the line.

Glue (or stitch) the tongue *behind* the face, so that it extends below as shown.

Glue (or appliqué) the brown eyes to the white pieces, with the pupils in the centre. Stitch the sequins to the pupils. Then glue (or appliqué) the eyes into position, following the pattern. Embroider all round the edge in stem (outline) stitch, using three strands of cotton (floss).

5 Pin the face to the head, over the inner edge of the fur. Appliqué into place (ignoring the tongue).

6 Right sides facing, oversew (overcast) the two head pieces together, leaving open between the notches across the top; tuck the fur down between the edges as you sew. Turn to the right side.

7 Fit the zip across the top and stitch it securely into place (turn under a very narrow hem at the back of the head, but stitch the fur-trimmed edge flat).

8 Cut the braid or cord to the required length for the strap, and stitch the ends securely at each end of the zip.

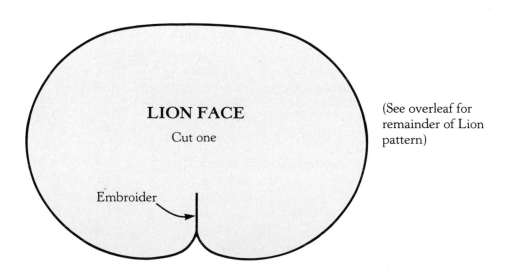

LION FACE

Cut one

Embroider

(See overleaf for remainder of Lion pattern)

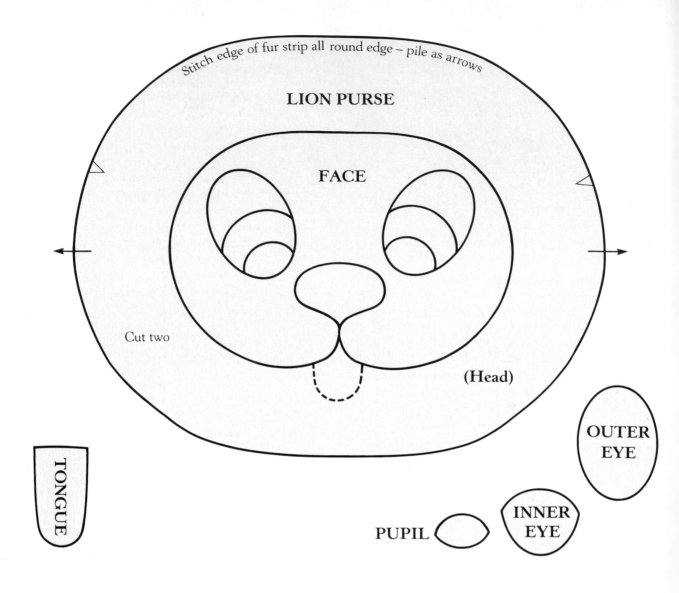

Stitch edge of fur strip all round edge – pile as arrows

LION PURSE

FACE

Cut two

(Head)

TONGUE

PUPIL

INNER EYE

OUTER EYE

FIVE FUN PENCIL CASES

Nearly all the decoration on these colourful pencil cases is bonded to the felt case with a hot iron. Although you can substitute glue if you prefer, take care with designs using fabric, because the bonding process seals the threads and prevents fraying edges. When bonding, don't forget that the design must be in reverse when you trace it.

The decoration is usually applied first, before the case is lined and made up. So run a tacking thread along the fold line of the felt square, so that when you open it out again, you can see exactly where to place your design so that it will be correctly positioned on the front half of the case. Remember that you must

allow also for the seams, so keep your distance from the edges too.

MATERIALS
20cm (8in) square of felt for the case
23cm (9in) square of medium-weight cotton-type fabric for the lining
Iron-on bonding material (Vilene Bondaweb or Pellon Wunder-Under)
10cm (4in) zip fastener
Matching threads
Decoration: see individual designs below

Green Pencil (dark green case)

DECORATION

5 x 15cm (2 x 6in) bright green felt
5cm (2in) square of camel felt
Scrap of black felt
Black stranded embroidery cotton (floss)

1 Following the instructions, trace and bond the main section of the pencil onto green felt. Then trace and bond the wood and lead onto camel and black felt respectively. Cut out.

2 Bond the camel wood under the green felt, then bond the black lead under the camel, placing the pieces over the pattern for guidance (take care to remove the backing paper only as far as the broken line; alternatively, if you find it easier, you can glue the pieces together).

3 Bond the complete pencil to the upper half of your prepared felt square, as illustrated.

4 Using three strands of cotton (floss), embroider the three equidistant lines on the pencil in stem (outline) stitch, as illustrated.

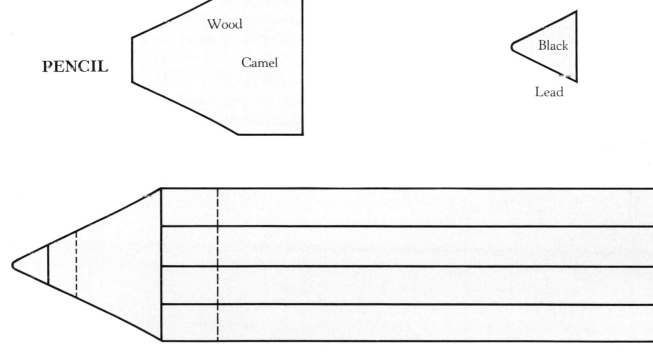

PENCIL

Wood
Camel

Black
Lead

Pencil

Green

Three Fish (aquamarine case)

DECORATION

12cm (5in) square of black felt
5cm (2in) square each: gold, cyclamen and lime-green felt
3 silver sequins, about 8mm (5/16in) diameter
3 smaller black sequins, about 5mm (3/16in) diameter
Small coloured sequins to tone with the coloured felts, about 5mm (3/16in) diameter
3 small black beads, about 5mm (3/16in) diameter
15cm (6in) metallic silver/black ribbon, 1.5mm (1/16in) wide
Black sewing thread

1 Following the instructions, trace and bond the outline of the *whole* fish three times onto black felt. Then trace and bond only the body once onto each of the coloured felts. Cut out.

2 Bond the bodies onto the black shapes. Then bond the three fish to the upper half of your prepared felt square, positioned as illustrated.

3 Stitch silver sequins into place for the eyes, with a smaller black one in the centre, as illustrated (the dot on the pattern marks the centres of the sequins). Stitch the beads into place for noses.

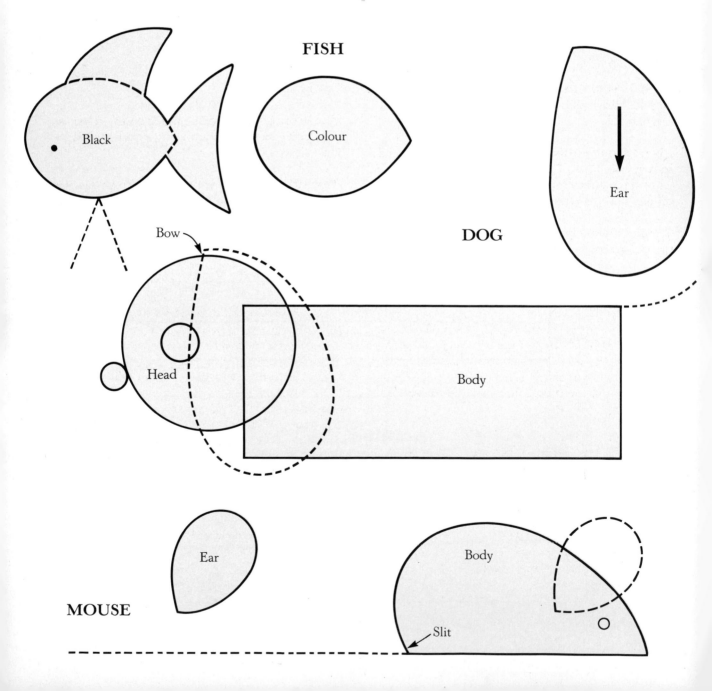

FISH

Black

Colour

DOG

Ear

Bow

Head

Body

MOUSE

Ear

Body

Slit

4 Stitch appropriately coloured sequins at random over each body.

5 Cut three 4cm (1½in) lengths of ribbon; fold each in half and stitch close under the body, as illustrated.

Pink Mouse (grey case)

DECORATION

5 x 8cm (2 x 3in) pink flowered medium-weight cotton-type fabric
Scrap of similar blue fabric for the ear
30cm (12in) pink satin ribbon, 1.5mm (¹/₁₆in) wide
15cm (6in) blue satin ribbon, 1.5mm (¹/₁₆in) wide
Black stranded embroidery cotton (floss)
Small black bead, about 5mm (³/₁₆in) diameter
Black sequin, about 5mm (³/₁₆in) diameter
Clear adhesive

1 Following the instructions, trace and bond the body onto the pink fabric and the ear onto the blue fabric. Cut out.

2 Bond the body to the upper half of your prepared felt square, about 2cm (¾in) above the fold line and (the nose) about 2.5cm (1in) from the left edge. Bond the ear into position on top.

3 Using three strands of cotton (floss), embroider round both pieces in stem (outline) stitch

4 Stitch the bead and sequin into place for the nose and eye.

5 Plait the ribbon (see Finishing Touches). Neaten the top of the plait for the tip of the tail, then make a tiny slit against the back of the body, as indicated, and thread the bottom of the plait through it. Glue the plait to the felt as indicated by the broken line, and as seen in the photograph.

Loopy Dog (blue case)

DECORATION

6 x 15cm (2½ x 6in) cream felt
Scrap of black felt
40cm (½yd) cream lampshade fringe, 2.5cm (1in) deep
5 x 7cm (2 x 2¾in) camel fur fabric
10cm (4in) pink single-face satin ribbon, 9mm (⅜in) wide
Black bead, about 7mm (¼in) diameter
Clear adhesive

1 Following the instructions, trace and bond the head and body separately onto the cream felt. Trace and bond the eye onto black felt. Cut out.

2 Bond the two cream pieces to the upper half of your prepared felt square, positioned as on the pattern.

3 Glue a row of fringe along the body, the lower edges of the fringe and body level. Add another row of fringe immediately above.
  Fold the top edge of the remaining fringe under, and lightly glue the loops down over it, to hold in place. Then glue this piece level with the top edge of the body, extending it as the broken line, for the tail.

4 Glue (or bond) the eye into position, following the pattern. And stitch the bead as indicated, for the nose.

5 Make up the case as directed below. Then complete steps 6 and 7.

6 Cut the ear in fur (the pile running down – as arrow), and glue it over the head and body, as indicated by the broken line.

7 Make the ribbon into a butterfly bow (page 9: points B 2.5cm [1in] from A). Glue to top of head and over ear, as illustrated.

To Make Up The Cases

Seam allowance: approximately 3mm (⅛in)

1 Place the felt and lining fabric wrong sides facing, and tack together all round the edge, keeping both absolutely smooth and flat.

2 Trim the fabric level with the edge of the felt.

3 Right side inside, fold the case in half and pin the long edge together. Beginning 1cm (⅜in) from the top (open) end, stitch securely together along this edge, turning the corner to join the short edge which will form the bottom end of the case.

4 Turn to the right side and press.

5 Stitch the zip fastener neatly into the top opening.

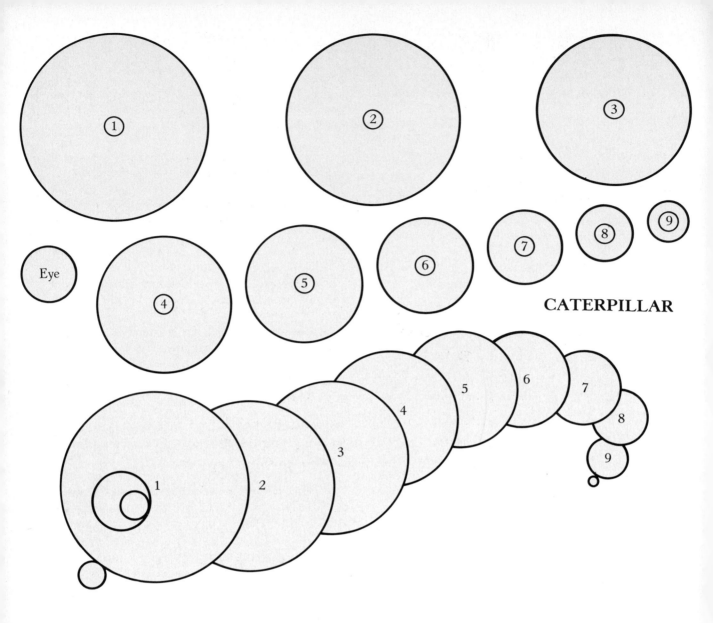

Eye

① ② ③

④ ⑤ ⑥ ⑦ ⑧ ⑨

CATERPILLAR

1 2 3 4 5 6 7 8 9

Curly Caterpillar (orange case)

DECORATION

15cm (6in) square of mid olive green felt
15cm (6in) square of light olive green felt
Scrap of bright yellow felt
Black bead, about 7mm (¼in) diameter
Black bead, about 5mm (³⁄₁₆in) diameter
Black sequin, about 8mm (⁵⁄₁₆in) diameter
Black stranded embroidery cotton (floss)

1 Following the instructions, trace and bond the circles onto felt squares; make the odd numbers mid olive, and the even numbers light olive. Trace and bond the eye onto the yellow felt. Cut everything out.

2 Place the olive circles on the upper half of your prepared felt square, overlapping and arranging them either as the outline pattern, or as you please. When you are satisfied with the result, bond the circles into position, adding the eye as illustrated.

3 Using three strands of cotton (floss), embroider an outline closely all round the caterpillar, and the eye, in stem (outline) stitch.

4 Stitch the sequin to the eye, as indicated.

5 Stitch the larger bead into place for the nose, and the smaller one for the tip of the tail.

The Bears' Story

PART FIVE

Greengage Bear was admiring the dolls which Banana Bear had just finished.

'How do you make them so soft?' he asked.

'With this lovely stuffing,' Banana Bear explained, showing him a big bag which he kept under his table.

Santa Claus was busy packing parcels to put on the sleigh. Greengage Bear thought this might be a good moment to approach him with the question they were all wanting to ask.

Greengage Bear cleared his throat. 'We want to know what you are going to do about the Christmas Mouse,' he said. 'It's always stealing our things. We all want to win the prize, but we can't do our best work when our materials keep disappearing.'

Santa scratched his head. 'Yes, I know it's a problem. I've told it off twice already, but it doesn't take any notice.'

They were interrupted by an angry shout from Banana Bear. 'Leave that bag alone!' he shrieked, as the Christmas Mouse scurried across the floor hugging a big bundle of fluffy white stuffing.

BANANA BEAR'S
Christmas Stocking Gifts

Bonnet Babies make an enchanting nursery or cradle decoration – and cry out to be adapted in so many different ways. Just sort through your odds and ends of fabric and trimming for inspiration. And, if you're in a Christmas rush, lots of charming but quick ideas for pretty packaging to make soaps and bath things special.

FOUR BABIES IN BONNETS

A very simple basic design, which lends itself to endless interpretation. Only tiny amounts of fabric are needed, so you should find lots of inspiration in your cuttings bag. The hair couldn't be easier, just a short length of purchased fringe. Choose from either the silky kind sold for lampshade-making, or thick-cut cushion fringe; see for yourself in the photographs, and notice how the cushion fringe also doubles as fur round the Eskimo baby's hood.

Following the basic doll, you will find full instructions for dressing Forget-me-not, the fair-haired baby in the flowery blue sunbonnet. Then see how easy it is to adapt the directions to make Blossom, the dark-haired babe in the pink and white robe; Daisy, the sultry beauty in country-style check gingham; and Nanook, cosily sewn into his colourful winter outfit.

The Baby

MATERIALS
18cm (7in) square of cream felt
Polyester stuffing
15cm (6in) silky lampshade fringe, or thick-cut cushion
    fringe, 2.5 (1in) deep
2 small brown or black sequins (see individual doll)
Matching and black threads

1 Cut the face once, and the body and head twice each.

2 Join the two head pieces to form the centre back seam, leaving open between the notches. Open out flat and join to the face, leaving the neck edge open between the lower notches. Turn to the right side.

3 Join the two body pieces, leaving the top and bottom

straight edges open. Push a knife handle or something similar up through the body until it protrudes about 2-3cm (an inch) above the edge of the neck; now fit the head over the handle and down over the neck until the lower edge is level with the broken line on the pattern. Stitch the head to the neck across the back only. Making tiny stitches close to the edge, gather across the neck edge of the face; draw up to fit, distributing the gathers evenly and stitch to the front neck.

4 Stuff the body quite firmly, up to the neck, then oversew the lower edges.

5 Stuff the head very firmly, beginning by pushing the stuffing down into the chin and lower part of the face, then pushing forward into the rest of the face from the back. Slip stitch the centre back seam.

6 Using double black thread, make a 3mm (⅛in) straight stitch at the centre of the face (about 4cm [1½in] below the seam) for the nose. Then, again with double thread, stitch a sequin at each side with eight stitches stretching beyond the edge of the sequin to form a star; position the sequins so that the centre is 1cm (⅜in) from the nose, and the lower edge level with it (see individual directions for Eskimo).

7 Without cutting the fringe, stretch 7cm (2¾in) across the forehead between the side seams, the centre falling 1cm (⅜in) below the seam at the top of the head; stitch into place. Then fold the remainder of the fringe back and take it over to the other side again, this time stitching it level with the seam.

Forget-Me-Not
Tiny blue flowers for a shady sunbonnet

The eyes are 5mm (³⁄₁₆in) diameter brown domed sequins. The hair is old-gold lampshade fringe.

MATERIALS
Lightweight blue flowered cotton-type fabric:
    dress: 15cm (6in) deep x 23cm (9in) wide
    bonnet: 12cm (4³⁄₄in) deep x 30cm (12in) wide
25cm (¹⁄₄yd) very narrow green broderie anglaise (eyelet embroidery) to trim hem
30cm (12in) white lace, 20mm (³⁄₄in) deep
1m (1yd) lilac lace, 10mm (³⁄₈in) deep
20cm (¹⁄₄yd) lilac single-face satin ribbon, 9mm (³⁄₈in) wide
Matching threads

1 Join the side edges of the dress fabric to form the centre back seam; press open. Turn up a 1.5cm (¹⁄₂in) hem and herringbone-stitch over the raw edge. Turn to the right side. Pin broderie anglaise inside the hem so that only about 1cm (³⁄₈in) emerges below; stitch into place.

2 Trim the skirt with a row of lilac lace, folded length-ways in half, and stitched 1cm (³⁄₈in) above the lower edge. Add two more rows, as illustrated, each 1cm (³⁄₈in) above the previous one.

3 Turn the top edge under and tack; then pin lilac lace around this edge to form a collar. Gather close to the top with double thread.

4 Fit the dress on the doll, seam at back, and draw up tightly round the neck.

5 Use the pattern (page 58) to cut and mark your bonnet fabric.

6 Fold back the brim as in figure 1; join each side between a-b. Clip the corners and turn the brim to the right side; tack, then press. Pin lace on top, as figure 2; gather between c-d, but don't draw up yet.

7 Join the lower edges between the notch (e) and the back edge (f); see figure 3.
    Gather the back edge and draw up as tightly as possible. Then gather the lower edge a-e-a, but don't draw up yet.

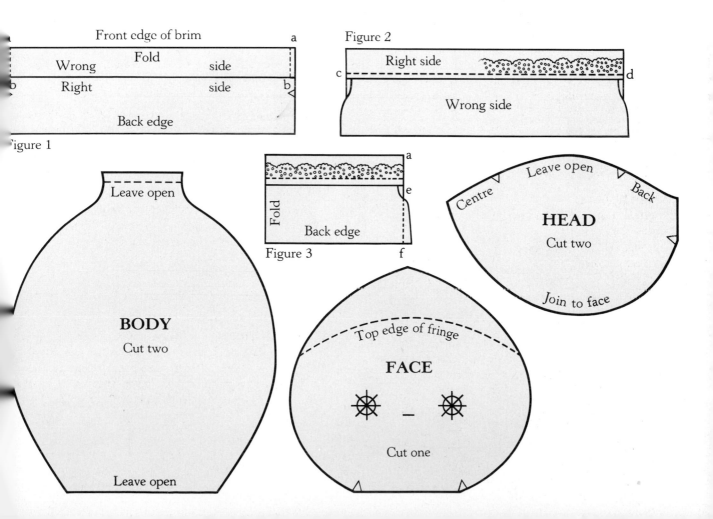

Figure 1

Front edge of brim   a

Wrong   Fold   side
b   Right   side   b
Back edge

Figure 2

Right side
c   d
Wrong side

Figure 3

a
Fold   e
Back edge
f

BODY
Cut two
Leave open
Leave open

HEAD
Cut two
Leave open
Centre   Back
Join to face

FACE
Cut one
Top edge of fringe

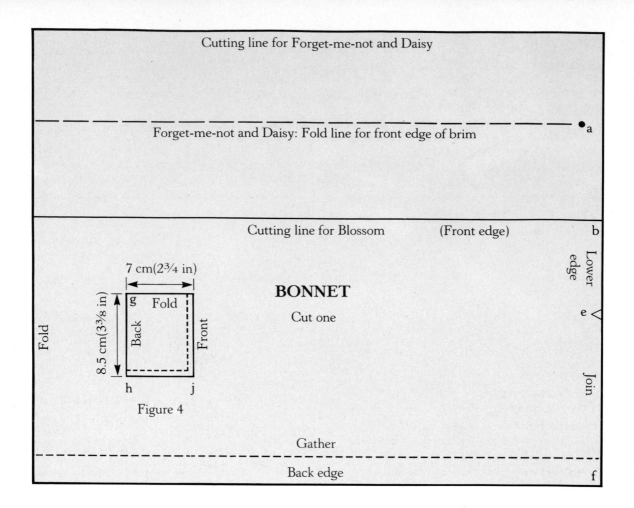

Cutting line for Forget-me-not and Daisy

Forget-me-not and Daisy: Fold line for front edge of brim •a

Cutting line for Blossom   (Front edge)   b

BONNET

Cut one

7 cm(2¾ in)

g   Fold

8.5 cm(3⅜ in)

Back   Front

Fold

h   j

Figure 4

Lower edge

e ∨

Join

Gather

Back edge   f

8 Fit bonnet on the head and draw up the lower gathers; stitch the corners (a) under the chin, 1.5cm (½in) apart.

9 Draw up the brim gathers over the hair and distribute them evenly, catching all round the head to hold in position.

10 Make a butterfly bow at the centre of the ribbon (see page 9: points B 2.5cm [1in] from A). Stitch between points marked a.

Blossom
Romantic pink bows and white lace trim a long robe

The eyes are 5mm (³/₁₆in) diameter brown domed sequins. The hair is dark brown lampshade fringe.

MATERIALS
Lightweight pink-and-white cotton-type fabric:
   dress: 20cm (8in) deep x 23cm (9in) wide
   bonnet: 7cm (2¾in) deep x 30cm (12in) wide
55cm (⅝yd) white lace, 20mm (¾in) deep
50cm (½yd) pink-and-white lace, 10mm (⅜in) deep

10cm (4in) pink single-face satin ribbon, 9mm (⅜in) wide
   (or use 6mm [¼in] wide)
35cm (⅜yd) pink single-face satin ribbon, 6mm (¼in) wide
Matching threads

1 As Forget-me-not, step 1, but instead of broderie anglaise, stitch a row of the wider lace around the hem, on the right side but close to the edge, so that most of the lace overlaps below.

2 Stitch a row of pink-and-white lace around the hem, just overlapping the top edge of the wide lace. Then add a second row so that it overlaps the top edge of the last one.
   Make four butterfly bows (see page 9) from 8cm (3⅛in) lengths of 6mm (¼in) ribbon; mark points B 2.5cm (1in) from A. Stitch one at the centre front of the skirt, over the top edge of the top row of lace. Stitch the others at approximately 4cm (1½in) intervals above the first one.

3 As Forget-me-not, steps 3 and 4, using pink-and-white lace for the collar.

4 Use the pattern to cut and mark your bonnet fabric, noting the cutting line for the front edge.

5 Turn under and tack a narrow hem along the front edge. Then pin wide lace on top so that most of it overlaps the edge. Gather the lace and fabric together, close to the folded edge, but don't draw up yet.

6 Complete the bonnet as Forget-me-not, steps 7-10 inclusive. If you haven't any wider ribbon to make the bow, use the same width as the bows on the dress.

Daisy
Fresh-as-a-daisy check gingham for that country look

The eyes are 5mm (³/₁₆in) diameter black domed sequins. The hair is black thick-cut cushion fringe.

MATERIALS

Brown-and-white check gingham:
    dress: 13cm (5in) deep x 23cm (9in) wide
    bonnet: 12cm (4¾in) deep x 30cm (12in) wide
Brown-and-white patterned cotton-type fabric for the underskirt: 18cm (7in) deep x 20cm (8in) wide
20cm (¼yd) white lace daisy trimming, 10mm (³/₈in) wide
50cm (½yd) very narrow white lace
50cm (½yd) brown ric-rac braid
15cm (6in) brown single-face satin ribbon, 6mm (¼in) wide
Matching threads

1 Make the underskirt as for Forget-me-not, step 1, but trim the hem with a row of ric-rac braid just above the edge.

2 Complete and fit the underskirt as steps 3 and 4 for Forget-me-not's dress, omitting the lace collar.

3 Join the side edges of the gingham to form the centre back seam. Press open. Make a narrow hem around the lower edge. Turn to the right side.

4 Turn the top edge over to the *right* side, to form a 1.5cm (½in) deep collar. Then gather close to the fold with double thread, but don't draw up yet. Stitch narrow lace over the raw edge of the collar.

5 Stitch ric-rac braid around the hem, *inside* the skirt so that only the lower half is visible. Then stitch narrow lace just above, as illustrated.
    Stitch lace daisies down the centre front.

6 Fit the dress on the doll and draw up tightly round the neck.

7 Make the bonnet as directed for Forget-me-not, steps 5-10, omitting the lace inside the brim, but when you gather the lower edge, *leave the brim free*, so that you catch the front corners to the doll at each end of the brim gathers. Add a band of lace daisies around the head over the brim gathers when the bonnet is completed.

Nanook
Cosy sleeping bag keeps a little Eskimo snug and warm

The eyes are 6-7mm (¼in) diameter black sequins, the lower half cut away just below the central hole. The hair is black lampshade fringe.

MATERIALS

Lime-green felt:
    bag: 12.5cm (5in) deep x 17cm (6¾in) wide
    hood: 7cm (2¾in) deep x 20cm (8in) wide
30cm (12in) brown thick cut cushion fringe
Toning and/or contrasting embroidered ribbon, ric-rac and dress braids to trim (see step 2)
Matching threads
Clear adhesive (optional)

1 Oversew the side edges of the bag to form centre back seam. Turn to the right side. Matching the centre back seam to the centre front, join the bottom; but before doing so, fit the fringe inside so that it protrudes as illustrated, then stitch felt to each side of the fringe.

2 Decorate with ribbon and braid trimmings; stitch and/or glue them into place, using the illustration for guidance.

3 Gather close to the top edge with a double thread. Fit the doll inside and draw up tightly round the neck.

4 Catch thick-cut fringe around the head, positioning it over the seam and then joining the ends under the chin.

5 Fold the hood in half and join the centre back seam g-h (figure 4). Gather close to the front edge j-j, but don't draw up yet. Gather the lower edge j-h-j; fit the hood on the doll and draw up these gathers round the neck, stitching the corners (j) under the chin below the fringe. Then draw up the front gathers over the back edge of the fringe, catching the felt to it to hold in place.

CLEAN AND FRESH AND FRAGRANT:
THE COTTAGE GARDEN EFFECT

Toiletries are always amongst the most popular gifts at Christmas-time. Everyone uses them – and a little luxury never did anyone any harm, so usually a gift of soap or something nice to put in the bath will be received with pleasure. Having said that, you can make a small and quite insignificant piece of soap or a bath cube look quite special with a little 'dressing-up'. The secret is to buy standard soaps, bath cubes or any other favourite toiletry and then pretty them up to look as romantic (and expensive) as you know how.

A glamorous presentation and trimming is the perfect disguise for all kinds of boring, but useful things – such as a collection of coloured cotton wool balls, a quite ordinary tin of talcum powder, a lipstick, a jar of face cream . . . even a bottle of skin tonic or old-fashioned rose-water. Or you could adapt the misty roses idea to surround a spoonful of pot-pourri, with a ribbon loop to hang it inside the wardrobe.

Why not seek your inspiration in a cottage garden, where silvery dew shimmers on rose petals in the early morning, butterflies flutter amongst the fresh green leaves, and fruit ripens in the sunshine. You can even hide a tablet of soap in the cottage itself.

Misty Rose Soaps

Small round guest soaps, delicately perfumed, are surrounded by frilled circles of fine net, with carefully matched satin roses nestling in the frothy gathers; the effect is enchanting.

MATERIALS
Round guest soaps (see below: step 1)
Fine net or tulle in white or a toning pastel shade
Single-face satin ribbon for roses (see below: step 3)
Single-face green (Spring Moss) satin, or silver grosgrain,
    ribbon for leaves (see below: step 4)
Matching threads
Clear adhesive

1 Use medium-weight waste paper to make your patterns. These will need to be adapted to fit your own tablets of soap, but for the 6cm (2¼in) diameter guest-size soaps illustrated, a 20cm (8in) diameter circle was used for the outer pattern, and a 13cm (5in) circle for the inner one.

2 Cut the larger circle in net. Pin and then tack the smaller pattern in the centre of the net. Gather close to the edge of the paper, then remove it (figure 1), place the soap in the centre and draw up the gathers tightly round it.

3 Choose ribbons which either match or tone with your soaps, and make roses as directed in Finishing Touches. The large single blooms are 30cm (12in) lengths of 12mm (½in) wide ribbon. Each miniature rose in the cluster of three is made from 15cm (6in) of 6mm (¼in) wide ribbon.

4 Make leaves as illustrated, and as described in Finishing Touches, using the patterns on this page. You will need 8cm (3in) of 23mm (1in) wide satin ribbon to make each large green leaf, or 3cm (1¼in) of 15mm (⅝in) wide grosgrain ribbon to make a smaller silver one.

5 Glue leaves behind the roses, then glue the rose in the centre of the gathered net, using a generous blob of glue and pressing the rose very firmly down into position, so that the frills are partially flattened.

Fragrant Fruits

These small novelty fruit soaps smell quite mouthwatering. Those illustrated are an apple, an apricot and a strawberry; they are 4-5cm (1½-2in) in diameter. With just a little 'fancy packaging', they make a charming tiny gift.

MATERIALS
Small 'fruit' soaps (see above)
Fine net or tulle in white or a toning pastel shade
Single-face green (Spring Moss) satin ribbon, 23mm (1in)
    wide, for the leaves
Scrap of natural garden raffia
Matching threads
Clear adhesive

1 Make the patterns as for the rose soaps (step 1), adjusting the size to suit your fruits. For the ones illustrated, a 15cm (6in) diameter outer circle was used, with a 10cm (4in) inner one.

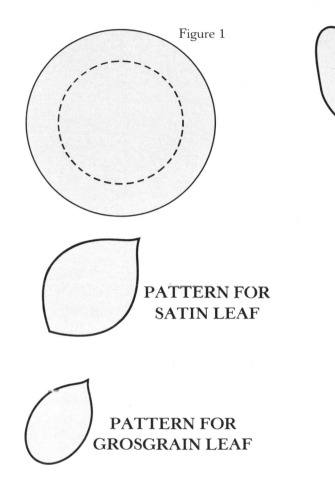

Figure 1

**PATTERN FOR
SATIN LEAF**

**PATTERN FOR
GROSGRAIN LEAF**

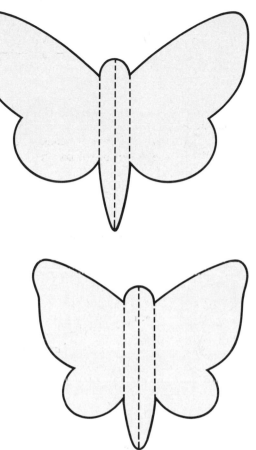

2 As step 2 for the rose soaps.

3 Tie a short length of raffia round, over the gathers, and trim the ends to leave about 2-2.5cm (¾-1in).

4 Make leaves as described in Finishing Touches, using the pattern on this page. Glue alongside the frills.

Beautiful Bath Cubes

Even a mundane bath cube can be given the beauty treatment – and emerge looking rather superior. Just buy a pleasantly scented packet of standard cubes, then re-wrap them in 7 x 15cm (2¾ x 6in) pieces of shimmering foil gift-wrap; the Hallmark paper shown has an attractive diagonal stripe.

Then it's back to the cottage garden for more roses (see the rose soaps above), adding a satin or grosgrain leaf before you glue the rose on top of the neatly wrapped cube. Or set the flower in a rosette of

gathered lace; join the cut ends of a 15cm (6in) length of 12-15mm (½-⅝in) wide lace, then gather the straight edge and draw up to leave a 1cm (⅜in) diameter hole in the centre.

If you'd like an alternative to roses, perch a delicate butterfly on the foil-wrapped cube. The one illustrated is also made from Hallmark gift-wrap – this time shimmering spots on a matt black ground create a dramatic butterfly that is very easy to make.

Trace the butterfly pattern and cut it out. Place your tracing over the gift-wrap and draw round the outer edge of the pattern. Back the butterfly with another piece of gift-wrap; smooth the paper carefully and leave under a heavy book to dry. Then cut it out.

Score the central broken line *on the back* with a blunt knife, then turn the butterfly over and score the other two broken lines on the front. Fold in half down the centre, creasing well, then fold the wings up along the two outer lines, creasing again. Holding the folded tail tightly, pull the head end of the body open again.

Fix in position with a blob of glue under the body.

Christmas Cottage: A gift of soap

A fragrant tablet of soap sits in the base of this festive cottage; the top is filled up with a few bubbles of bath oil. Any soap will do, simply adjust the measurements of your cottage to fit. But it's important to use a good quality wrapping paper to cover it – like the Hallmark Christmas gift-wrap illustrated.

MATERIALS
Thin card
Christmas gift-wrap paper
Hallmark white Curl-sheen gift-wrap ribbon *or* cotton wool
Dry-stick adhesive
Clear adhesive

1 The cottage illustrated is built around a 125gm tablet of soap packed in a box measuring 9 x 6.5cm (3½ x 2½in). Measure your own box and, if it differs, adjust the measurements of the pattern pieces accordingly, adding a little extra – about 5mm (¼in) – so that the soap fits inside easily. If you are adapting the patterns, copy the existing ones onto graph paper, then adjust the measurements accordingly to make your own patterns. You won't need to alter the height – just the width of the side and end; then make the base conform to the same measurements. Adjust the width and depth of the roof so that it fits on top with a good overlap all round. The only other slight adjustment necessary will be the two inverted V-shapes at the base of the chimney; to get the correct angle, place the top of your end pattern over the chimney pattern and draw round it.

2 Cut the side and end twice each in card, and the base, roof and chimney once each.

3 For the existing pattern cut a piece of gift-wrap 36cm (14¼in) wide x 11cm (4¼in) deep. If you have adjusted the pattern, add the width of your two sides and two ends together and add 3cm (1¼in) for the width, but cut the paper the same depth.

4 Stick the sides and ends smoothly to the back of the paper as figure 1; allow a fraction of space between the pieces – about 1mm (¹⁄₃₂in). Make three cuts in the gift-wrap at the top, as indicated, and cut away the shaded areas.

5 Fold the sides and ends round and glue the overlapping paper (A) behind the other end, to join. Slip the base inside, and then the soap; fold up the overlapping paper below each end (B) and glue under the base. Then glue the overlap below the sides (C) underneath the base in the same way.
   Fold back the triangles D at the top of the ends, then fold back pieces E and glue them to D.
   Fill up with bath oil bubbles, or alternative.

6 Score the roof as indicated, then cover it with gift-wrap, allowing an overlap of about 1.5cm (½in) all round; snip off the corners, then turn the surplus underneath and glue down neatly.
   Bend the roof over and glue it to E on each side of the cottage.

7 Score the chimney as indicated, then cover it with gift-wrap, ignoring the tab, but *don't* cut away the inverted V-shapes at the base; cut this paper as figure 2, then bend the triangles back and use them to glue the chimney to the centre top of the roof.

8 Curl a metre (yard) of the ribbon as instructed, and glue inside the chimney – or use cotton wool.

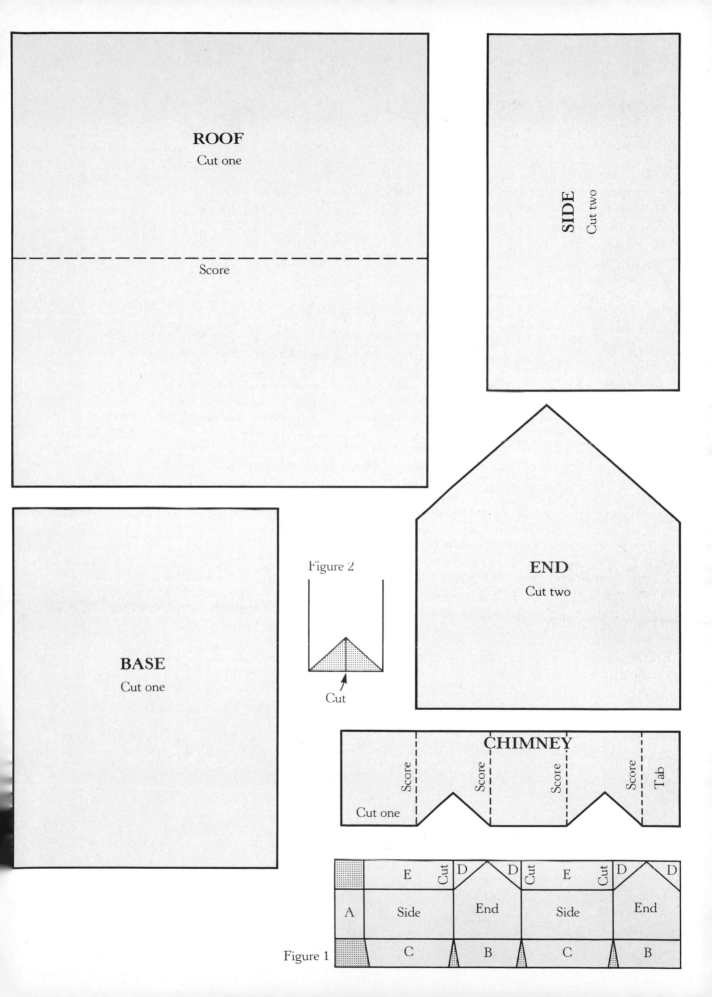

ROOF

Cut one

Score

SIDE

Cut two

BASE

Cut one

Figure 2

Cut

END

Cut two

CHIMNEY

Score   Score   Score   Score   Tab

Cut one

	E	Cut	D		D	Cut	E	Cut	D		D
A	Side		End		Side		End
	C	B	C	B

Figure 1

The Bears' Story

PART SIX

Santa was snoozing in his armchair. He had worked hard, reading children's letters and checking them against the list of presents in his ledger, packing parcels, working out his route on the map, and doing all the hundred-and-one things that were necessary before midnight. Now he had ten minutes for a brief nap.

Greengage Bear was congratulating Blueberry Bear on his pincushions. 'How do you get the owl's eyes to sparkle so?' he asked.

'With sequins,' Blueberry Bear explained, showing him a collection of little boxes. Greengage Bear exclaimed in delight at the shiny round sequins, which shimmered and sparkled as they caught the light.

'They're lovely!' breathed Greengage Bear. 'I wish I had some!'

'Ask Santa,' suggested Blueberry Bear, 'I'm sure he'd give you a box.'

As the two bears walked across to Santa's armchair, they heard a slight movement behind them. They turned to look, and stared in horror as the Christmas Mouse dashed towards its hole, clutching a small round box – of Blueberry Bear's best gold sequins!

BLUEBERRY BEAR'S
Christmas Stocking Gifts

Three quite different cuddly bunnies — all from the same pattern. Simple to make, but a lovely gift to charm both small children and customers alike. Useful pincushions in the shape of amusing patchwork characters, double as paperweights if you want them to.

THREE BABY BUNNIES

Everyone's idea of a cuddly bunny. The perfect gift for a baby. And a gift to sew and stuff too. No need to worry about hiding your stitches when you sew up the seam after stuffing — because there's no seam to sew up. Simply gather the top edge of the body . . . and gather the lower edge of the head . . . then ladder-stitch the two together. If you've never ladder-stitched before, you'll find clear instructions on page 7.

There are three versions to choose from; two show ways to combine contrasting furs, whilst the other uses only one fur. Present them just as they are, or dress them up with a big satin bow — or a feminine bonnet trimmed with ribbons and lace.

MATERIALS

20cm (8in) blue-grey fur fabric,70cm (28in) wide (A)
20cm (8in) silver-grey fur fabric, 60cm (24in) wide (B)
12cm (4¾in) white fur fabric, 11cm ((4½in) wide (B)
20cm (8in) camel fur fabric, 50cm (20in) wide (C)
12cm (4¾in) cream fur fabric, 22cm (9in) wide (C)
8 x 15cm (3 x 6in) heavy Vilene or Pellon non-woven interlining
Scraps of black and pale pink felt
Polyester stuffing
Fluffy white knitting yarn (or purchased pompon)
Matching threads
Thin card (for pompon)
Fine string (for pompon — if necessary)
Clear adhesive

1 For version A, cut the head gusset, chest and base once each, the face and body twice each (reversing each pattern to cut the second piece), and the ear four times, all in blue-grey fur fabric.

Note: approximately 5mm (³/₁₆in) is allowed for seams. Work with right sides together and sew with a back-stitch unless otherwise directed. (See notes on cutting fur fabric: page 6.)

Amounts of fur fabric are given for three versions:
   A: All blue-grey
   B: Silver-grey with white chest
   C: Brown with cream chest and ears

For version B, cut the head gusset and base once each; the face and body twice each (reversing each pattern to cut the second piece), and the ear four times, in silver-grey fur fabric. Cut the chest in white.

For version C, cut the head gusset and base once each; the face, body and ear twice each (reversing the pattern to cut the second face and body), in camel fur fabric. Cut the chest once and the ear twice more, in cream.

For all three versions, cut the base twice more in interlining, slightly smaller, as broken line on pattern.

2 Join the two pieces between A-B.

3 Cut the eyes in black felt (see cutting circles: page 6). Push a pin through the marked point on each side of the face, then push back the fur all round it and place the felt eye centrally on the point of the pin: push it down into position and appliqué or glue it into position. (If preferred, you can leave the eyes until the toy is finished.)

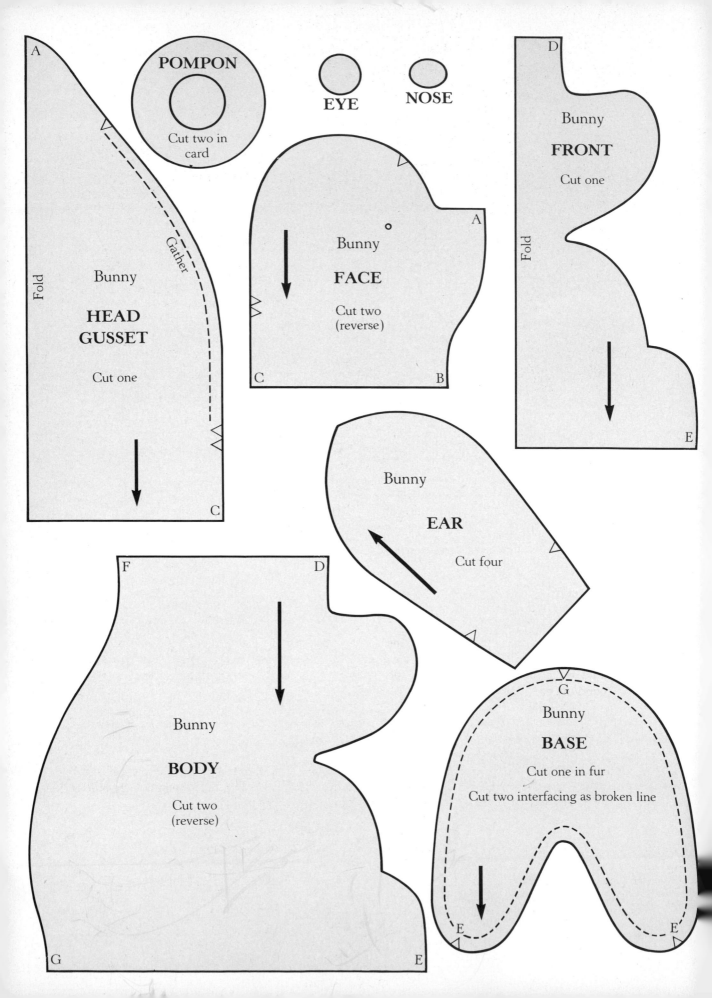

A

POMPON

Cut two in card

EYE

NOSE

D

Bunny

FRONT

Cut one

Fold

E

Fold

Gather

Bunny

HEAD GUSSET

Cut one

C

Bunny

FACE

Cut two
(reverse)

A

C

B

Bunny

EAR

Cut four

F

D

Bunny

BODY

Cut two
(reverse)

G

E

Bunny

BASE

Cut one in fur

Cut two interfacing as broken line

G

E

E

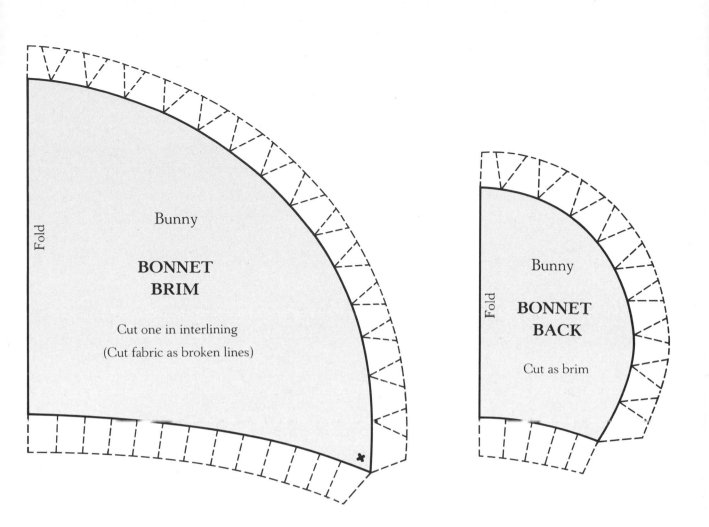

Fold

Bunny

**BONNET
BRIM**

Cut one in interlining

(Cut fabric as broken lines)

Fold

Bunny

**BONNET
BACK**

Cut as brim

4 Carefully match the tip of the head gusset (A) to the top of the seam: then join it to each side of the face between A and the single notch (it is important to do this little bit round the nose very accurately).

Join the other end of each seam between C and the double notch. Then gather each side of the gusset between the single and double notches. Pin the gusset to the face at each side, drawing up the gathers as you do so and distributing them evenly along the length of the seam, easing the gusset in to fit round the top of the face. Stitch securely over the gathers. Turn to the right side.

5 Stuff the head quite firmly, pushing the filling well up into the nose and chin. Using a double thread, gather round the lower edge of the head, then draw up tightly and secure.

6 Tack the double thickness of interlining to the wrong side of the base (use matching thread and try not to let your stitches show on the right side).

7 Join the body pieces to each side of the chest between D-E. Then join the centre back seam of the body (F-G).

8 Pin, and then stitch, the base to the lower edge of the body; match the notches to the seams as indicated. Turn to the right side.

9 Stuff the body as the head, then gather round the top edge and draw up securely as before.

10 Ladder-stitch the head and body together (see page 7).

11 To make each ear, *oversew* (overcast) two pieces together all round, leaving the straight lower edge open. Turn to the right side.

12 Pin the ears halfway down the back of the head, the outer edges just inside the edge of the gusset. Check the position from the front, then stitch securely into place with a darning needle, across the raw edges at the bottom and up each side to the notch.

13 Cut the nose in pink felt and glue into position over point A, where the gusset joins the two face pieces. Glue the eyes into place if you have not already done so.

14 Cut two circles of card as the pattern and make a pompon (see Finishing Touches), for the tail. Stitch to the body near the bottom of the back seam.

Bow

50cm (½yd) feather-edge double-face satin ribbon, 15mm (⅝in) wide

1 Tie tightly around the neck in a bow as illustrated, cutting the ends neatly in an inverted V-shape.

Bonnet

15cm (6in) medium-weight cotton-type fabric, 60cm (24in) wide
12 x 30cm (4¾ x 12in) heavy Vilene or Pellon non-woven interlining
Iron-on bonding material (Vilene Bondaweb or Pellon Wunder-Under) (optional – see step 1)
35cm (14in) very narrow lace
70cm (¾yd) very narrow dress or lampshade braid (see step 5)
1.2m (1⅜yd) single-face satin ribbon, 12mm (½in) wide, for the roses
30cm (12in) single-face satin ribbon, 9mm (⅜in) wide, for the ties
Matching threads
Clear adhesive

1 Cut the brim and back once each in interlining. Following the instructions on the pack, bond both pieces to the wrong side of your fabric, leaving at least 1cm (⅜in) surplus all round. (If you have no bonding material, use either dry-stick adhesive or glue; or

simply tack the two pieces together close to the edge.) Cut the fabric as shown by the outer broken lines on the patterns, snipping the surplus into small tabs, as indicated. Turn the tabs neatly over the edge of the interlining and glue them to the other side. Now cover this side with fabric in the same way, but this time trim it level with the edge of the interlining.

2 *On the right side*, oversew (overcast) the back edge of the brim round the upper edge of the back, matching the corners.

3 Stitch (or glue) lace around the inside of the brim, overlapping beyond the edge as illustrated.

4 Cut the narrow ribbon in half and stitch each piece inside the brim at X for the ties.

5 Glue braid all round the outer edge of the brim and back, and also over the join. (Use the narrowest braid you can find: either cut narrow dress or lampshade braid down the centre [as illustrated] or make your own plaited braid – see Finishing Touches.)

6 Make three roses (see Finishing Touches), using 40cm (16in) ribbon for each. Stitch to the top of the bonnet as illustrated.

PATCHWORK AND PINCUSHIONS

When you're 'idea-hunting' for small gifts which are not only attractive, but useful too, there are some perennial favourites that immediately spring to mind. And when you stop to think about it, you realise that they owe their enduring success to the fact that they are fun to make, fun to give and fun to receive. Novelty pincushions are high on the list, and the designs shown on page 66/7 combine some amusing plump pets with another popular medium – patchwork. However, the patchwork used here isn't the conventional kind; it's a shameful cheat, designed for those in a hurry, to speed up what is usually a rather time-consuming process.

Hunt through your piece bag for patterned fabrics that go well together. Or, treat yourself to some specially designed patchwork fabrics like those used for the examples illustrated. You will need only to buy the smallest amount, so you can choose an artistic selection without spending a lot of money. And then the fun starts, because the tiny designs are so pretty that you'll be inspired to do all kinds of exciting things as well as patchwork.

To make paperweight pets, insert a smooth stone or similar object when stuffing.

Patchwork Pincushion

MATERIALS
Medium-weight firmly woven cotton-type fabric in four (or more) designs, for the patches (see step 1)
20cm (8in) square of felt in a toning colour
Iron-on bonding material (Vilene Bondaweb or Pellon Wunder-Under)
Matching or toning thread
Polyester stuffing
Stiff card
30cm (12in) toning braid, about 10mm (³⁄₈in) wide
Clear adhesive

You can, of course, prepare your patches and sew them together in the traditional way. But if you want to cheat, here's how to do it.

1 Trace the outline of the patch onto Bondaweb or Wunder-Under. Following the instructions on the pack, iron the tracing onto the wrong side of your fabric, first checking that the design on the fabric is positioned as you want it. Cut the patch out and back it with felt, as instructed; then cut the felt absolutely level with the fabric.

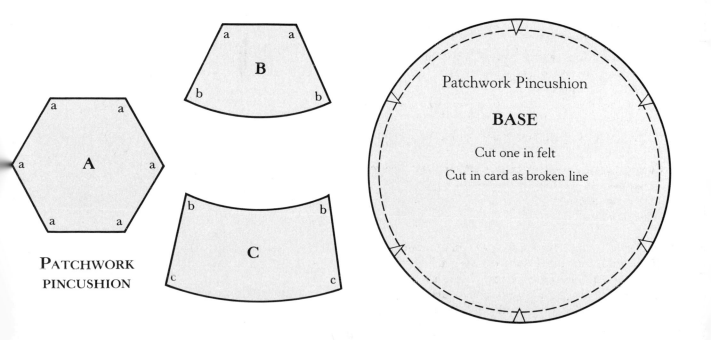

PATCHWORK
PINCUSHION

You will probably enjoy working out your own patchwork arrangement, but if you want to follow the one illustrated on page 66/7, prepare patch A once in your first fabric; prepare patch B six times in your second fabric; and prepare patch C three times each in your third and fourth fabrics.

2 Right sides together, oversew (overcast) each B patch to patch A, matching the points marked a (make sure the edge of the fabric is caught securely in the seam).

3 Alternating the fabric designs, sew the C patches to the B patches, matching the points marked b.

4 Now join all the patches between a-b-c, matching the corners carefully. Turn to the right side and gather close to the lower edge, but don't draw up yet.

5 Cut the base in felt; then follow the broken line to cut a slightly smaller circle of stiff card. Glue the card to the felt. Mark the edge of the felt into six equal sections, as notches.

6 With the card inside, pin the patchwork to the base, matching the end of a seam to each marked point. Draw up the gathers to fit and oversew (overcast) neatly together all round, leaving one section open.

7 Stuff the pincushion very firmly indeed, then finish sewing the edges together.

8 Glue braid neatly round the edge of the base to mask your stitches.

Pincushion Owl

MATERIALS
20cm (8in) square of burgundy felt
Medium-weight firmly woven cotton-type fabric for eyes
Medium-weight firmly woven cotton-type fabric for chest
Iron-on bonding material (Vilene Bondaweb or Pellon Wunder-Under)
Polyester stuffing
2 large black domed sequins, about 8mm ($^5/_{16}$in) diameter
Stranded black embroidery cotton (floss)
Matching threads

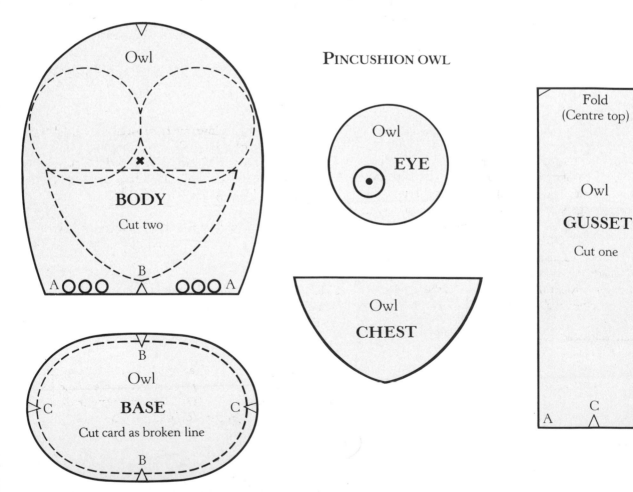

PINCUSHION OWL

Large wooden bead, about 10mm (⅜in) diameter, for beak
6 small wooden beads, about 5mm (³⁄₁₆in) diameter, for feet
Stiff card
Clear adhesive (optional)

1 Cut the body twice, and the gusset and base once each, in felt. Cut the base again, slightly smaller as the broken line, in card.

2 Trace the eye twice and the chest once, onto Bondaweb or Wunder-Under and, following the instructions on the pack, iron them onto the wrong side of your chosen fabrics and cut out the shapes. (If your fabric is very thin, it can be a good idea to back the eyes with felt at this stage, but a firm fabric should not need backing.)

3 Using three strands of black embroidery cotton (floss), buttonhole stitch around the edge of the eyes. Stitch the sequins into place for the pupils, as indicated on the pattern.

4 Carefully position the chest on one body piece, as indicated on the pattern, then iron it into place, following the instructions. Bond the eyes into position in the same way. (If you have backed your pieces with felt, glue them into place instead.)

5 Right sides together, oversew (overcast) the gusset strip all round the upper edge of the body front, matching points A and centres. Then join the second body piece to the other side of the gusset in the same way.

6 Pin the base round the lower edge, matching the notches to the centres of the body front and back (B), and the gusset at each side (C). Stitch together around both gusset edges and the front, but leave the back open between A-A. Turn to the right side.

7 Slip the card base inside and pin it into position from outside (hold in place with a little glue, if you wish). Stuff the owl very firmly, then slip-stitch the edges together across the back.

8 Stitch the bead beak into position in the space between the eyes and chest (X on pattern). Then stitch three small beads at each side of the lower edge of the front, as indicated, for his feet.

Pincushion Pig

MATERIALS
20cm (8in) square of raspberry-coloured felt
Flower-patterned light blue medium-weight firmly woven cotton-type fabric for the ears
7 x 10cm (2¾ x 4in) light blue felt to match fabric
Scrap of pink felt for the nose
Iron-on bonding material (Vilene Bondaweb or Pellon Wunder-Under)
Polyester stuffing
Stranded blue embroidery cotton (floss) to match ears
Stranded black embroidery cotton
7cm (2¾in) pipe cleaner (chenille stem)
Matching threads
Stiff card
Clear adhesive

1 Cut the body twice, and the base and tail once each, in raspberry felt. Cut the base again in card, slightly smaller, following the broken line.

2 Trace the ear twice onto Bondaweb or Wunder-Under *reversing the second one*. Following the instructions on the pack, iron the tracings onto the wrong side of your fabric and cut out. Then back with blue felt, as instructed, and trim the felt absolutely level with the fabric.

Using three strands of blue embroidery cotton (floss), buttonhole-stitch all round the edge of each ear.

3 With right sides facing, oversew (overcast) the body pieces together between A-B.

Join the base to each side of the body, matching points B-C, but leaving open at the back between the notches. Turn to the right side.

4 Cut the nose in pink felt and carefully fit it into position, then buttonhole-stitch it into place with matching sewing thread.

5 Slip the card base inside and pin temporarily from outside (hold in place with a little glue, if necessary). Stuff the pig very firmly, then slip-stitch the edges neatly together.

6 Pin the ears to the body as illustrated, to help determine the position of the eyes; mark the curved line indicated with pins and, when you are happy with them, embroider them in stem (outline) stitch, using three

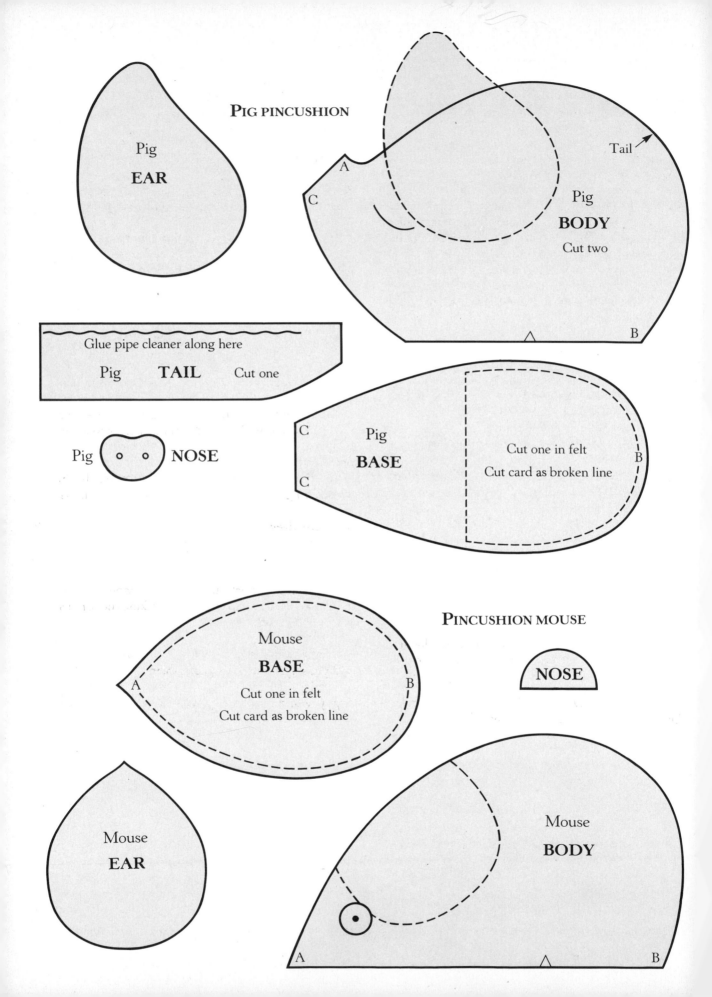

PIG PINCUSHION

Pig **EAR**

Pig **BODY**

Cut two

Tail

A

C

B

Glue pipe cleaner along here

Pig **TAIL** Cut one

Pig **NOSE**

C

Pig **BASE**

Cut one in felt

Cut card as broken line

C

B

Mouse **BASE**

Cut one in felt

Cut card as broken line

A

B

PINCUSHION MOUSE

NOSE

Mouse **EAR**

Mouse **BODY**

A

B

strands of black embroidery cotton (floss) (hide the ends of your cottons behind the ears).

Stitch the ears into place.

7 Embroider two French knots on the nose, as indicated on the pattern.

8 Glue the pipe cleaner (chenille stem) close to the longer edge of the tail, as indicated. Then, beginning at the narrow end, roll the felt tightly round the cleaner and slip-stitch the edge to hold it in place.

Using the points of your *closed* embroidery scissors, ease a gap in the seam at the point indicated on the body pattern, then insert the end of the tail and stitch it securely into place.

Pincushion Mouse

MATERIALS

15cm (6in) square of mid-blue felt
Flower-patterned pink medium-weight firmly woven cotton-type fabric for the ears
6 x 10cm (2½ x 4in) pink felt to match the above fabric
Scrap of black felt
Iron-on bonding material (Vilene Bondaweb or Pellon Wunder-Under)
Polyester stuffing
15cm (6in) matching blue lacing cord (*or* 15cm [6in] pipe cleaner [chenille stem]: see step 6)
2 large black domed sequins, about 8mm (5/16in) diameter
Stranded pink embroidery cotton (floss) to match ears
Matching threads
Stiff card
Clear adhesive

1 Cut the body twice and the base once, in blue felt. Cut the base again, slightly smaller as shown by the broken line, in card.

2 Trace the ear twice onto Bondaweb or Wunder-Under. Following the instructions on the pack, iron the tracings onto the wrong side of your fabric and cut out. Then back with pink felt, as instructed, and trim the felt absolutely level with the fabric.

Using three strands of pink embroidery cotton (floss) buttonhole-stitch all round the edge of each ear.

3 With right sides facing, oversew (overcast) the curved upper edge of the body together between A-B.

4 Pin the base round the lower edge, matching points A and B. Stitch together, but leave open at the back between the notches. Turn to the right side.

5 Slip the card base inside, pinning temporarily from the outside (hold in place with glue if necessary). Then stuff the mouse very firmly and slip-stitch the edges neatly together at one side, between the notch and the seam.

6 Make a knot at one end of the lacing cord and slip it inside the body below the seam, so that the rest of the cord extends behind the body for the tail; stitch it securely into place, then complete slip-stitching the edges of the body and base together.

Cut the tail to the length required, then seal the tip by smearing it with a little adhesive and twisting it to a point between the fingertips.

Alternatively, make an extended version of the pig's tail (step 8), using a pipe cleaner (chenille stem) and a 2 x 16cm (¾ x 6½in) strip of felt.

7 Cut the nose in black felt and glue it smoothly round point A at the front tip of the body, taking the corners neatly underneath.

8 Pin the ears to the sides of the head as illustrated, and pin sequins just in front of them, as indicated, to determine the position of the eyes. When you are happy with these, stitch the sequins into place. Then stitch the ears into position.

The Bears' Story

PART SEVEN

The workshop was in chaos. Everything was turned upside-down and the bears were all crawling round under their benches looking into the bags and boxes.

Santa stood in the middle of the workshop, watching the bears keenly. He was nearly ready to leave for his long journey through the cold night sky, cosily dressed in his fur-trimmed red suit. But his feet were bare, and he held his boots in his hand. Because he couldn't find his socks!

The bears had searched everywhere, but in vain.

Raspberry Bear had been making tea cosies all day, and as he was peering inside each one, just in case, a flash of red caught his eye. He turned sharply towards the Christmas Mouse's hole.

Something like a long, lumpy, red-and-white striped sausage was stuck in the mousehole. It was one of Santa's socks.

RASPBERRY BEAR'S
Christmas Stocking Gifts

With grown-ups – and especially grandparents – in mind; tea cosies to make tea-for-one more enjoyable, and fishy oven mitts to prevent burnt hands when they're in and out of the oven. Smartly personalised cases protect specs, whether they're sunglasses or the reading kind and, for avid readers, a selection of bookmarks add a twist to the tale.

THREE TEA-FOR-ONE TEA COSIES

The photograph on page 78/9 shows three different versions of the all-round cosy. The first, in a bold flower-garden printed cotton in strong colours, needs no additional decoration. The country-fresh pink gingham cosy is edged with crisp white ric-rac, and has three deeper pink roses nestling under the frill. And the pretty white flower print on a pale coffee ground, with a plain lining the colour of strong black coffee, has a creamy coffee satin bow for a final touch of sophistication.

MATERIALS
35cm (⅜yd) medium-weight cotton-type fabric, 90cm (36in) wide *or* 20 x 65cm (8 x 26in) *each* in two fabrics (for lined cosy)
20 x 60cm (8 x 24in) wadding, 4oz thickness
1m (1yd) white ric-rac braid (gingham cosy)
2m (2¼yd) single-face satin ribbon, 9mm (⅜in) wide, for roses
60cm (24in) double-face satin ribbon, 15mm (⅝in) wide, for bows
2 snap fasteners
Matching threads

Seam allowance: approximately 7mm (¼in)

1 For either the flower-garden cosy, or the pink gingham, cut the cosy pattern four times in fabric, and the base and frill A twice each.

For the plain and pretty lined version, cut the cosy pattern and frill B twice in each fabric, and the base once in each fabric.

2 Following the broken line, cut the cosy twice, and the base, once, in wadding.

3 *Frill A:* fold one strip in half lengthways, right side inside, and stitch the ends. Clip the corners, turn to the right side and press.

Frill B: right sides together, join two frill strips, one in each colour, along the top edge and both ends. Clip the corners, turn to the right side and press.

4 Gather the raw edge of the strip. Pin the frill to the right side of one outer cosy piece, raw edges level and matching notches. Draw up the gathers to fit, distributing them evenly, and stitch.

5 Repeat steps 3 and 4 for the second frill.

6 Tack wadding to the wrong side of the inner cosy pieces. Pin a padded piece to each frilled piece, right sides together. Stitch all round the curved edge; clip the seam and turn to the right side. Turn in the raw lower edge and tack. Then catch the wadding to the lining with a row of small stitches near the lower edge.

7 Tack wadding to the wrong side of one base circle. Then join to the other piece, right sides together, leaving 5cm (2in) open. Clip the seam, then turn to the right side. Turn in the raw edges and slip-stitch together.

8 Right sides together, pin the lower edge of each side of the cosy around the base, corners meeting. Oversew together, then turn the stitching inside the cosy.

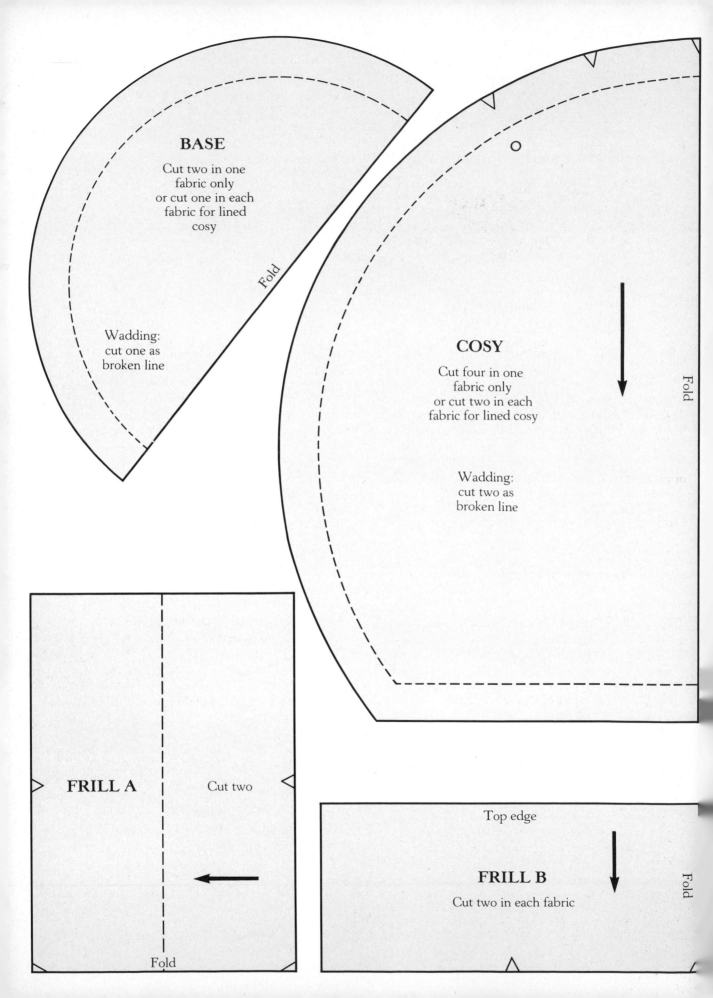

BASE

Cut two in one
fabric only
or cut one in each
fabric for lined
cosy

Fold

Wadding:
cut one as
broken line

COSY

Cut four in one
fabric only
or cut two in each
fabric for lined cosy

Fold

Wadding:
cut two as
broken line

FRILL A

Cut two

Fold

Fold

Top edge

FRILL B

Cut two in each fabric

Fold

9 Top-stitch round each side, close to the edge, inside the cosy.

10 Stitch a snap fastener inside the cosy, just below each end of the frill (points marked o on pattern).

11 For the gingham cosy, stitch ric-rac around the curved edge on each side, as illustrated.

Make two roses (see Finishing Touches) from 40cm (16in) ribbon each, and four roses from 30cm (12in)

each. Stitch one large rose over the ric-rac, below the centre of the frill, with a smaller one on each side.

12 For the lined cosy, cut the ribbon in half and make a formal bow (see Finishing Touches) for each side from a 15cm (6in) length, bound with a piece 3cm (1¼in) long, with ties (streamers) made from the remaining 12cm (4¾in). Stitch to the cosy, just below the centre of the frill, as illustrated.

TWO PAIRS OF PISCES OVEN-MITTS

If you enjoy the sheer pleasure of needlecraft, you'll have as much fun sewing this fishy design, as the eventual owner will when it's swimming in opposite directions round the kitchen. It's also a nice one for children to do, because there's plenty of variety, not too much of anything for it to become boring, and no difficult operations.

The fact that it is practical as well as amusing, makes the Pisces pair a doubly acceptable gift. On the other hand, it can be made almost entirely from leftovers and oddments, so it's ideal if the cost of materials has to be balanced against profits.

MATERIALS
Two 35 x 20cm (14 x 8in) pieces of fabric for top sides of fish
Two 35 x 20cm (14 x 8in) pieces of fabric for undersides of fish
Two 15 x 20cm (6 x 8in) pieces of felt for heads and tails, in colours to tone with the top fabric
6 x 12cm (2⅜ x 4¾in) white felt for eyes
3 x 6cm (1¼ x 2½in) black felt for pupils
8cm (3in) square of pink felt for noses
20 x 65cm (8 x 26in) thick wadding
20cm (8in) bias binding in shades to match or tone with each head felt
50cm (⅝in) black ric-rac braid
2 coloured sequins, about 8mm (⁵⁄₁₆in) diameter
Black stranded embroidery cotton (floss)
Matching threads

Seam allowance. 5mm (³⁄₁₆in)

1 Cut the fish shape twice in each fabric. Cut the head and tail once in each felt. Cut the eye twice in white felt, the pupil twice in black, and the nose twice in pink.

2 Right sides together, join the two pieces of fabric you are using for the plain underside of the fishes (these can be the same or contrasting – see the illustration on page 78/9), along the straight tail ends. Press the seam open. Join the other two pieces of fabric in the same way, *but only with a tacking thread*. When you have pressed it open, tack the edges of this seam down at each side.

3 Place your wadding on the wrong side of the first piece of fabric (the underside) and tack together, keeping them both smooth and flat.

4 Bind the straight edge of each head piece. Then stitch ric-rac over the edge of the binding.

5 Appliqué the nose and eye into position on each head piece.

Buttonhole stitch all around the eye, using three strands of embroidery cotton.

6 Place the heads in position at each end of the second (un-padded) piece of fabric (wrong side of head to right side of fabric); tack together.

7 Place the two pieces of fabric right sides together and tack quite close to the edge. Stitch firmly together all

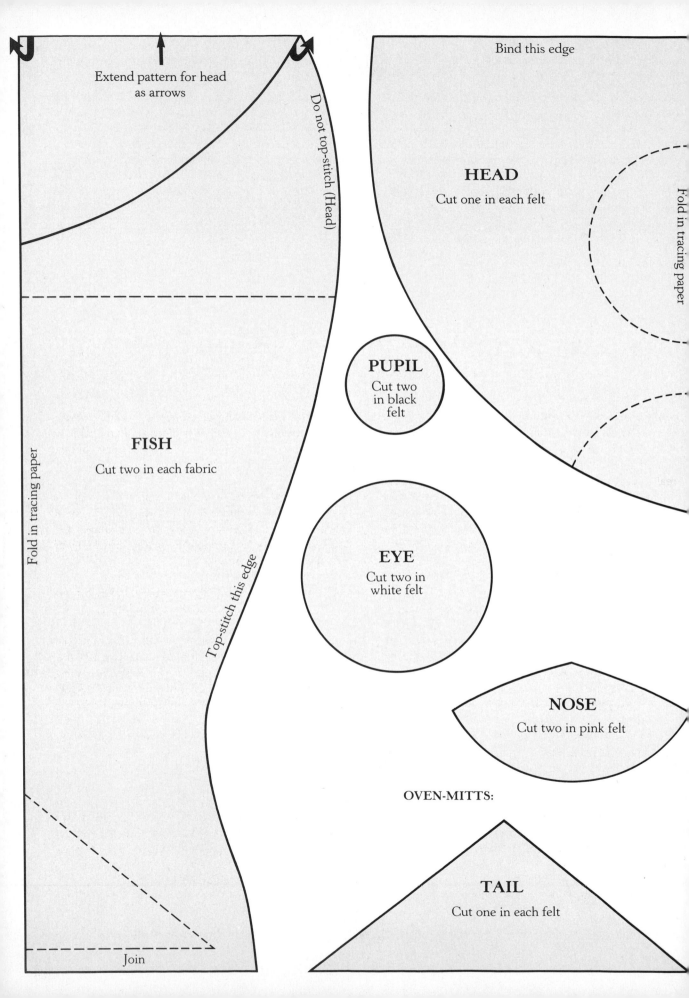

Extend pattern for head
as arrows

Do not top-stitch (Head)

Bind this edge

HEAD

Cut one in each felt

Fold in tracing paper

PUPIL

Cut two
in black
felt

Fold in tracing paper

FISH

Cut two in each fabric

Top-stitch this edge

EYE

Cut two in
white felt

NOSE

Cut two in pink felt

OVEN-MITTS:

TAIL

Cut one in each felt

Join

round the edge, then trim close to the seam with pinking shears.

8 Pull out the central tacking thread between the tail ends, and carefully turn everything to the right side, then slip-stitch the edges together again. Remove the other tacking threads and appliqué the tail pieces into position, the straight back edge against the seam.

Stitch ric-rac braid over the join.

9 Top-stitch all round the edge of the *fabric* only, not the heads. Then press.

10 Pin the pupils in position, then appliqué, adding the sequins as a final highlight.

SEVEN CASES FOR SPECTACLES AND SUNGLASSES

Soft but protectively firm, you can use this basic pattern as a springboard for endless ideas of your own. Anyone who wears spectacles or sunglasses needs somewhere to keep them, so these smart cases make a really practical gift, whether you're giving or selling. If they're for family or friends, make the decoration something very personal to the individual concerned. If you're planning your sales' policy, then go for novelty, whether it be pretty or witty.

MATERIALS
18cm (7in) square of felt for case
18cm (7in) square of matching, toning or contrasting felt for lining
17cm (6⅝in) square of Vilene or Pellon non-woven interlining
Iron-on bonding material (Vilene Bondaweb or Pellon Wunder-Under)
Firm, closely-woven, medium-weight cotton-type fabric for decoration
Other items for decoration, as necessary (see individual designs)
Matching threads
Clear adhesive

1 If you are *not* using one of the designs shown here, trace the shape of the pattern onto graph paper and work out your own design to scale, so that you can trace it off accurately.

2 Cut your outer felt to size (metric or imperial measurements – as above), using the pattern to round off the corners (cut one corner only top and bottom; then fold the felt in half and cut the second corners level with the first ones).

3 Decorate the front of the case in your own way, or following the individual directions below; it is important to do any bonding at this stage, but additional decoration, or glued items, may be done when the case is finished.

4 Using the pattern for guidance, round off the corners of the interlining as you did the felt in step 2.

5 Spread glue along the top edge of the interlining and round the top corners; dot a little more glue here and there over the rest of the piece. Turn the interlining over and press it smoothly down on the lining felt, then cut the felt level with the edge of the interlining.

6 Glue the other side of the interlining exactly as you did the first side, then press it smoothly down on the back of the outer felt, leaving an equal overlap all round.

7 Fold the case in half and oversew (overcast) the edges together very neatly down the side below the x (reinforcing well at that point), and across the bottom. If sewing by hand, work back again over your first row of stitches, for added durability.

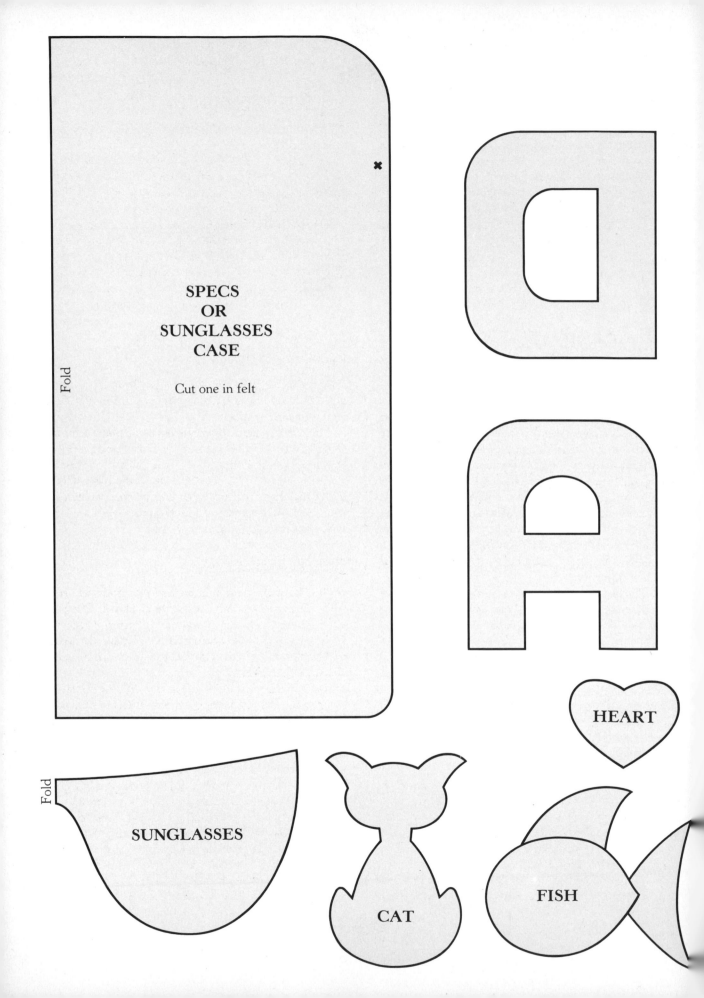

**SPECS
OR
SUNGLASSES
CASE**

Cut one in felt

Fold

Fold

SUNGLASSES

CAT

HEART

FISH

Dad's Specs Case

Using a ruler to ensure your lines are absolutely straight and accurate, trace two Ds and one A (note Ds are reversed) onto your Bondaweb or Wunder-Under. Taking care to match any pattern very carefully, and following the instructions on the product, iron the tracing onto the back of your fabric. Then cut the letters out. Peel the paper off the back of the fabric and place the letters very carefully in the required position on the felt for the case. Place a hot iron on top for just a moment to anchor them in position, then press with a damp cloth, as instructed. Leave until cool and dry, then continue to step 4 above.

Mum's and Gran's Specs Case

Rule the 18 x 9cm (7 x 3½in) outline shape of the case on a piece of household greaseproof paper, or good quality tissue. Place this over a sheet of graph or squared paper, and draw out the appropriate letters exactly as you wish them to fall on the case. Find an attractive embroidered or lace trimming and experiment with it over your pencil letters to see how well it will work. You may need to adjust the size or shape of your letters to accommodate the decoration better.

When you are satisfied, tack the tracing to your case, matching the edges of the pattern to the edges of the felt. Now stitch very carefully and accurately through the paper, making small, neat running stitches along the pencil lines. Tear the paper away very gently, so that the design is neatly stitched on the felt. Glue the trimming very accurately over the stitched lines, then leave the felt under some heavy weight for an hour or two before continuing as step 4 above.

Flowery Sunglasses Case

Trace the design onto Bondaweb or Wunder-Under as described for Dad's case (but no need to reverse anything). Bond the flowered fabric to the case in exactly the same way.

The frame in the illustration is made from a plaited ribbon braid (see Finishing Touches) that echoes three shades from the flower print, taking 50cm (20in) of each 1.5mm (¹⁄₁₆in) wide satin ribbon. This is glued over the cut edge of the fabric, all round the lower edge of the sunglasses. Above is a band of wide ric-rac braid, picking out the green of the print, with the braid mounted on top; cut 15cm (6in) ric-rac to length, turning under the cut ends. Continue as step 4 above.

Satin Hearts Case

Any scraps of satin would do — or you could use another kind of fabric with an interesting texture; the example shown uses scraps of single-face satin ribbon, in a rainbow selection of colours. Equally effective, though, would be alternating hearts in light and dark shades of just one colour, on a contrast ground.

Once you've decided how you are going to interpret the design, just trace the required number of hearts onto Bondaweb or Wunder-Under, then bond them to your satin or alternative fabric, and cut out. Arrange the hearts on your felt in any way you please, then bond them into place and complete the case as step 4 above.

Cat Silhouette Case

Trace the cat onto Bondaweb or Wunder-Under, bond it to black felt and cut it out. Bond it to your felt as illustrated.

Plait three 12cm (4¾in) lengths of black 1.5mm (¹⁄₁₆in) wide satin ribbon (see Finishing Touches) for the tail. Trim the top end to a neat point for the tip of the tail. Make a tiny slit close under the base of the body, slip the other end of the plait up through it, and catch behind the body to hold it securely in place.

Complete the case as step 4 above.

Sparkly Fish Case

Trace the complete outline of the fish onto Bondaweb or Wunder-Under and prepare in black felt. Prepare the body only in the same way, using a scrap of satin to tone with the colour of your case. Bond the body to the black felt, then bond the whole fish to your case, positioning as illustrated.

Decorate with sequins, using a small black one in the centre of a larger one for the eye, and small ones in two or three toning colours to cover the rest of the body; stitch them all into place with fine black sewing thread. Add a small black bead for the nose.

Plait three 12cm (4¾in) lengths of 1.5mm (¹⁄₁₆in) wide satin ribbon (see Finishing Touches), each in a different colour to tone with the fish (the one in the photograph has a fin plaited from red, orange and metallic gold ribbons). Trim the top end to a neat point for the tip of the fin. Make a tiny slit close under the base of the body, slip the other end of the plait up through it, and catch behind the body to hold it securely in place. Finish the case as step 4 above.

TEN TWIST-IN-THE-TALE BOOKMARKS

Just a few ideas to set you thinking . . . Every reader needs something to mark the place, and these are much smarter than a used envelope or an old bus ticket! Odd scraps of felt and fabric combine with ribbons, braid and a few sequins to make some amusing and original markers. Patterns for the ones shown in the photograph are all here, with details of how they were done – but you've probably volumes of far more exciting ideas of your own.

Sleek Black Cat

MATERIALS

9 x 6cm (3½ x 2½in) black felt

Iron-on bonding material (Vilene Bondaweb or Pellon Wunder-Under)

Stiff black paper or thin card

15cm (6in) heavy black ric-rac braid

60cm (¾yd) black satin ribbon, 1.5mm (¹⁄₁₆in) wide *or* 20cm (¼yd) each of three colours

Ribbon or braid for collar (optional)

Adhesive tape

Clear adhesive

1 Following the instructions on the product, trace the cat onto Bondaweb or Wunder-Under and bond it to the black felt. Cut out and bond the other side to the paper or card. Cut out.

2 Plait the ribbon neatly (see Finishing Touches), then trim the top end to a neat point for the tip of the tail. Glue the plaited ribbon to the braid, keeping it absolutely central. Trim the braid neatly to match the pointed end of the plait.

3 Glue the other end of the tail to the back of the mark, reinforcing it with a tiny piece of tape over the top.

4 If you wish, glue a collar around the neck, cut ends at the back. The one illustrated is 1.5mm (¹⁄₁₆in) metallic gold/blue ribbon, plaited as for the tail.

Never-Forget Elephant

MATERIALS

8 x 10cm (3 x 4in) patterned medium-weight cotton-type fabric

7cm (2¾in) square of toning felt

Iron-on bonding material (Vilene Bondaweb or Pellon Wunder-Under)

Stiff paper or thin card (ideally in a toning shade)

30cm (12in) satin ribbon, 1.5mm (¹⁄₁₆in) wide in *each* of three colours matched to the patterned fabric

Clear adhesive

1 Following the instructions on the product, trace the whole outline of the elephant, and then the body only,

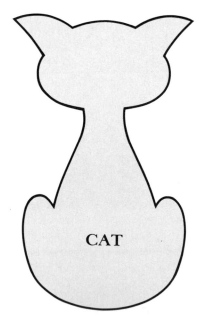

CAT

onto Bondaweb or Wunder-Under; bond the whole outline to the patterned fabric and the body onto felt. Cut out.

2 Bond the body into position on the fabric, then bond the fabric to the paper or card. Cut out.

3 Plait the ribbons (see Finishing Touches), making a knot at the bottom of the plait for the tip of the tail; trim the ends neatly.

4 Glue the top of the plait firmly to the body at X.

Swimming Fish

MATERIALS

8 x 9cm (3 x 3½in) black felt

6 x 7cm (2½ x 2¾in) patterned medium-weight cotton-type fabric

Iron-on bonding material (Vilene Bondaweb or Pellon Wunder-Under)

Stiff black paper or thin card

30cm (12in) satin ribbon, 1.5mm (¹⁄₁₆in) wide in *each* of three colours matched to the patterned fabric

Large coloured sequin, about 8mm (⁵⁄₁₆in) diameter

Small black sequin, about 5mm (³⁄₁₆in) diameter

Fine black sewing thread

Adhesive tape

Clear adhesive

1 Following the instructions on the product, trace the outline of the whole fish, and then the body only, onto Bondaweb or Wunder-Under; bond the whole outline to the black felt and the body onto the fabric. Cut out.

2 Bond the body into position on the felt, then bond the felt to the paper or card. Cut out.

3 Stitch the large sequin into place for the eye, with the smaller one on top.

4 Plait the ribbons (see Finishing Touches), trimming the top of the plait to a neat point for the tip of the fin.

5 Glue the other end of the plait to the back of the mark, reinforcing it with a tiny piece of tape over the top.

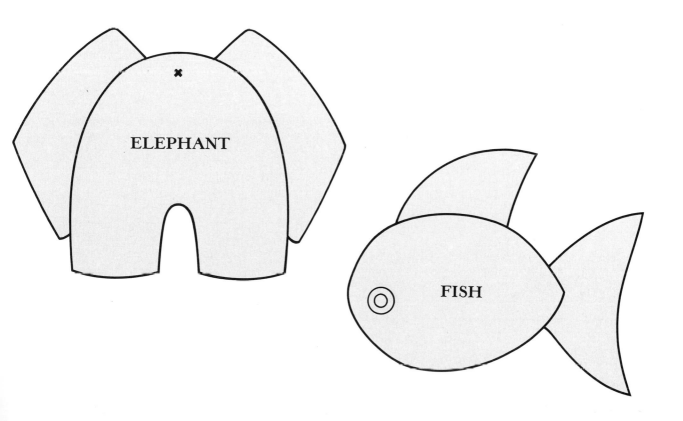

ELEPHANT

FISH

Wiffle the Mouse

MATERIALS

5 x 8cm (2 x 3in) patterned medium-weight cotton-type
   fabric
Scrap of toning fabric or felt for the ear
Iron-on bonding material (Vilene Bondaweb or Pellon
   Wunder-Under)
Stiff paper or thin card (ideally in a toning shade)
60cm (24in) and 30cm (12in) satin ribbon, 1.5mm (1/16in)
   wide, in colours to tone with the fabric and felt
Small black sequin, about 5mm (3/16in) diameter
Fine black sewing thread
Adhesive tape
Clear adhesive

1 Following the instructions on the product, trace the
body and the ear separately onto Bondaweb or
Wunder-Under; bond to the appropriate fabrics or felt
and cut out.

2 Bond the body to the paper or card, then bond the
ear into position on top. Cut out.

3 Stitch the sequin into place for the eye.

4 Plait the ribbons (see Finishing Touches), then trim
the top end to a neat point for the tip of the tail.

5 Glue the other end of the plait to the back of the
mark, reinforcing it with a tiny piece of tape over the
top.

Love Story

MATERIALS

7 x 9cm (3 x 3½in) patterned medium-weight cotton-type
   fabric
Iron-on bonding material (Vilene Bondaweb or Pellon
   Wunder-Under)
Stiff paper or thin card (ideally in a toning shade)
20cm (¼yd) satin ribbon, 1.5mm (1/16in) wide in *each* of
   three colours matched to the pattern on the fabric
40cm (½yd) ric-rac braid to match background of fabric
Adhesive tape
Clear adhesive

1 Following the instructions on the product, trace the
heart onto Bondaweb or Wunder-Under and bond it
to the fabric. Cut out and bond the other side to the
paper or card. Cut out.

2 Glue ric-rac neatly all round the edge of the heart,
sticking it to the *back* of the card, so that barely half the
width of the braid is visible.

3 Plait the ribbon (see Finishing Touches), then trim
the top end to a neat point for the tip. Glue the plaited
ribbon to a 20cm (8in) length of the remaining ric-rac,
keeping it absolutely central. Trim the end neatly, to
match the pointed end of the plait.

4 Glue the other end of the braid-backed plait to the
back of the mark, reinforcing it with a tiny piece of
tape over the top.

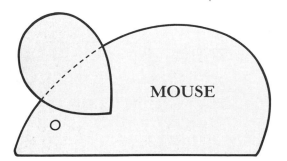

MOUSE

HEART

The Bears' Story

PART EIGHT

Santa's sock was firmly wedged, but Raspberry Bear tugged very hard and finally it came out.

Santa stood in front of the hole. 'Christmas Mouse,' he boomed, 'Where is my other sock?'

There was a long silence. Then the mouse slowly emerged, one small paw trailing the missing sock. 'I'm sorry, Santa,' it sobbed, 'But I wanted to enter the competition for the Best Christmas Stocking.'

'Well next time borrow someone else's stocking,' grunted Santa, thrusting his foot into one of the socks. 'Ouch!' he exclaimed, withdrawing his foot quickly, 'There's something inside!' He lowered his hand gingerly into the sock . . . and pulled out a tiny figure of a shepherd carrying a baby lamb. Then he pulled out a richly dressed king, followed by two more kings and another shepherd . . . and finally, Mary and Joseph and the Infant Jesus.

The bears gasped in admiration as Santa set the perfect little figures down on a bench. They formed a beautiful Nativity scene, and the bears recognised all the things they had lost.

'I think,' Santa said slowly, turning to the circle of bears, 'We're all agreed about who has won the prize?'

The bears nodded happily, Then they all started clapping and cheering.

Santa told the Mouse to find a warm cloak while he looked for a cushion to make it comfortable on the sleigh.

Just after midnight Santa and the little mouse joined the bears to sing carols around the candlelit Nativity scene. Then they tiptoed away and set off together for a night the Christmas Mouse would never forget.

THE NATIVITY
Angelica's Christmas Crib

All the adult figures are developed from the basic velvet tubing figure used for the 'One-Plus-One Makes Partners' characters. As you may not wish to have the complete Nativity scene, materials are given separately for the different characters. For instance, you might want to make only a simple crib with just Mary, Joseph and the Infant Jesus – or the three main characters and one or two shepherds – or perhaps just the Three Kings, as a distinctive table decoration.

First decide which characters you are going to make, checking to note the colour of the Offray velvet tubing used for each one; then turn to the list of materials on page 12 to calculate the amounts of velvet tubing, heads, hands and feet, and pipe cleaners (chenille stems), you will need.

Colours and decoration will be your own decision. The directions below describe the figures illustrated, and the colour-schemes are specified simply to make identification easier. Instructions are given for those trimmings used, in case you wish to copy any of them yourself. But your own characters' dress should be dictated by your personal taste and available materials; so *your* figures will look quite different – and probably even more imaginative.

MATERIALS
For all the characters
Twilley's stranded embroidery wool, or fine knitting yarn, for hair and beards
Matching threads
Tiny pins
Sepia or black pencil or pen
Clear adhesive

Joseph and the Shepherds
10 x 12.5cm (4 x 5in) medium-weight cotton-type fabric for the robe (see step 1)
10 x 16cm (4 x 6½in) medium-weight cotton-type fabric for the outer garment (see step 1)
12 x 16cm (4¾ x 6½in) medium or lightweight cotton-type fabric for the head-cloth
11cm (4½in) square of felt in a toning or neutral shade to back the robe

Iron-on bonding material (Vilene Bondaweb or Pellon Wunder-Under) or dry-stick adhesive
60cm (24in) satin ribbon, 1.5mm (¹/₁₆in) wide, for each girdle (see step 4)
60cm (24in) satin ribbon, 1.5mm (¹/₁₆in) wide, for each headband (see step 6)
Thin twig or stick, about 10cm (4in) long, for each shepherd's staff
3 white pompons, 1.5cm (½-⅝in) diameter, for the lamb
Scraps of white felt and cotton wool (absorbent cotton), for ears and tail
3 tiny black beads, for the lamb's features
Gold sequin, 3cm (1¼in) diameter (hole near edge, if possible), for Joseph

The Virgin Mary
14 x 12.5cm (5½ x 5in) medium-weight cotton-type cream fabric for her robe and headband
14 x 27cm (5½ x 10½in) medium-weight cotton-type blue fabric for her shawl
Gold sequin, 3cm (1¼in) diameter (hole near edge, if possible)
Stiff card, 10cm (4in) deep x about 5cm (2in) wide

The Infant Jesus
Turned paper, or alternative, craft ball, 1.5cm (⅝in) diameter, flesh-tinted, or painted with poster colour
Pipe cleaner (chenille stem), 8cm (3in) long
Cotton wool (absorbent cotton)
10cm (4in) square of medium-weight, cotton-type, cream fabric
Gold sequin, 1.5cm (⅝in) diameter (hole near edge, if possible)

The Three Kings

11cm (4½in) squares of felt in green, blue and violet for their robes, *plus* a 7cm (3in) circle of violet for the crown

10cm (4in) circle of gold felt for the turban

10 x 45cm (4 x 18in) or a 25cm (10in) square of black felt for *all three* cloaks

90cm (1yd) satin ribbon, 1.5mm (¹⁄₁₆in) wide, *in each of three colours* to make plaited braid *for each king*

35cm (⅜yd) very narrow braid in a dark toning colour or black, for each king (optional)

15cm (6in) very narrow silver or gold ric-rac braid to trim each robe

12cm (5in) lengths of gold braid, tiny beads, etc, for crown (see step 24)

20cm (8in) green velvet tubing for turban

30cm (12in) dark blue or black velvet tubing for steeple

Small piece of medium-weight white paper

Small piece of blue (or silver) foil paper

Polyester stuffing or cotton wool (absorbent cotton)

Tiny star sequins in assorted colours and silver and gold

3 coloured glass Christmas tree baubles, about 2cm (¾in) diameter, for their caskets (see step 26)

Tiny silver, gold, coloured and pearl beads, diamanté (rhine-stones) etc, and 3 larger coloured beads, to decorate the head-dresses and caskets (see steps 23, 25 and 26)

Joseph and the Shepherds

1 Following the directions on page 12, make Joseph in brown (or black) velvet tubing; make one shepherd in scarlet, and the other in emerald.

All wear the basic robe, with a sleeveless outer garment over it. Use a plain mid-brown fabric for both of Joseph's garments. Find two matching and/or toning fabrics for each shepherd; in the illustration, the scarlet shepherd has a scarlet striped robe with a dark brown outer garment, and the emerald shepherd wears a green and brown multi-check robe with a woven green outer garment. For all these garments, it is important to choose fabrics that won't fray (unravel) too much; but a firmly woven fabric will result in a *slightly* frayed edge, which emphasises the fact that these characters are poorly dressed.

2 Trace the robe onto Bondaweb or Wunder-Under and, following the instructions on the product, bond it to your fabric. Cut it out, cutting slits for the armholes. Then bond the other side to your felt, as instructed, and cut it out again. (Alternatively, use a glue-stick to back the fabric with felt.)

Right side inside, oversew (overcast) the straight edges together to form the centre back seam. Turn to the right side. Fit on the figure and glue or stitch the top corners together over each shoulder.

3 Cut the outer garment in your chosen fabric, cutting slits for the armholes. Fold the front edges under along the broken lines, pin but do not crease. Fit the garment on the figure and join the top corners over each shoulder. Draw the garment back at each side and glue the folded-under corners to the robe to hold in place.

4 Plait three 20cm (8in) lengths of ribbon (see Finishing Touches) to make a 15cm (6in) long girdle. Glue the ends and trim neatly, then circle the hips as illustrated, catching at the front to hold in place.

5 To make each beard, tie twenty-five 8cm (3¼in) lengths of wool tightly at the centre with a single strand. Fold in half and glue to the centre of the face, as illustrated. Trim to shape.

6 Cut the head-cloth in the appropriate fabric and make another length of plaited braid as the girdle, for the headband, using colours to match or tone with the other garments (see the illustration).

Drape the fabric over the head as illustrated, pinning it temporarily to hold it in place whilst you fit the headband; pin the headband too, arranging the gathers underneath and, when you are satisfied with both, catch the headband to the head with matching thread to hold it and the fabric in position.

7 To make the lamb, glue two pompons side-by-side, pushing them together for the body. Then glue on the third for the head, angling it as figure 1.

Cut the ear twice in white felt, and glue to sides of head. Glue on three tiny beads for the eyes and nose, as figure 1.

Twist a tiny scrap of cotton wool (absorbent cotton) for the tail, and glue into position.

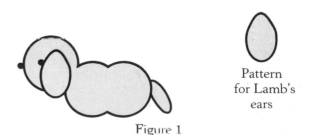

Figure 1

Pattern for Lamb's ears

Tuck the lamb under a shepherd's arm, bending the hand round underneath to support its body.

8 Glue a thin twig or stick to each shepherd's hand, for his staff.

9 Pin the gold sequin to the back of Joseph's head, as illustrated, for his halo.

The Virgin Mary

10 Make the figure in white velvet tubing, following the directions on page 12.

11 Cut the robe and headband in cream fabric. Cut slits in the robe for the armholes. Overlap and glue the straight edges to form centre back join. Fit on the figure, glue top corners together over shoulders.

12 For the hair, wind two 76cm (30in) strands of embroidery wool around a 10cm (4in)-deep piece of card. Slip short pieces of wool under the loops and tie them together tightly at each edge. Slip off the card and tie the skein loosely at the centre.
   Glue the tied centre to the top of her head, then take each side down and round to the back, gluing lightly; twist each end before pinning to the nape of the neck.

13 Cut her shawl in blue fabric, cutting the straight edge along the thread. Fold the cream headband in half along the broken line, and press the fold. Spread glue lightly over one side of this strip, *leaving 3cm (1¼in) free at each end*; stick the strip to the straight front edge of shawl, on inside, centres matching and fold level with cut edge of shawl (see pattern).

14 Glue the back edge of the strip to the top of the head and pin the ends to the back of the head over the hair. Then fold the sides of the shawl so that it falls forward as illustrated, gluing it lightly in position.
   Drape the shawl round the body of the kneeling Virgin Mary, gluing lightly, or pinning, to hold in place (study the photograph for guidance).

15 Pin sequin to back of head, as illustrated.

The Infant Jesus

16 Bend the pipe cleaner (chenille stem), in half, and push the cut ends up into the head ball. Wrap cotton wool (absorbent cotton) round the pipe cleaner to form the body.

17 Cut fifteen 5cm (2in) lengths of wool. Tie them tightly at the centre, then fold in half and glue the tied section to the back of the head, so that the strands come forward, covering the top and sides of the head, and the cut ends surround the face.

18 Place the fabric wrong side uppermost and fold the top corner (A) over as figure 2. Then place the figure centrally on top. Bring the folded edge round the head and catch together tightly under the chin; then over-sew (overcast) the folded edges together down the centre front over the body. Bring corner B up and catch to the bottom of the front seam. Now wrap the fabric tightly round the body, sewing it neatly to hold in position. Trim the hair to length round the face, and pin the sequin halo to the back of the head.

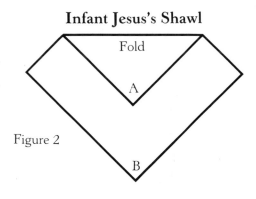

Infant Jesus's Shawl

Figure 2

The Three Kings

19 Make all three figures in black velvet tubing, following the directions on page 12.

20 Cut the robe in coloured felt, cutting slits for the armholes. Oversew (overcast) the straight edges to form the centre back seam.
   Make plaited braid (see Finishing Touches) from 90cm (1yd) of ribbon in each of three toning shades. Glue around the hem of the robe, level with the cut edge. Glue a band of silver or gold ric-rac braid immediately above, then add another row of plaited braid immediately above the ric-rac. Glue coloured stars over the lower half of the robe, at the front only. Fit robe, joining top corners over the shoulders.

21 Cut the cloak in black felt. Glue the remaining plaited braid all round the outer edge, including the

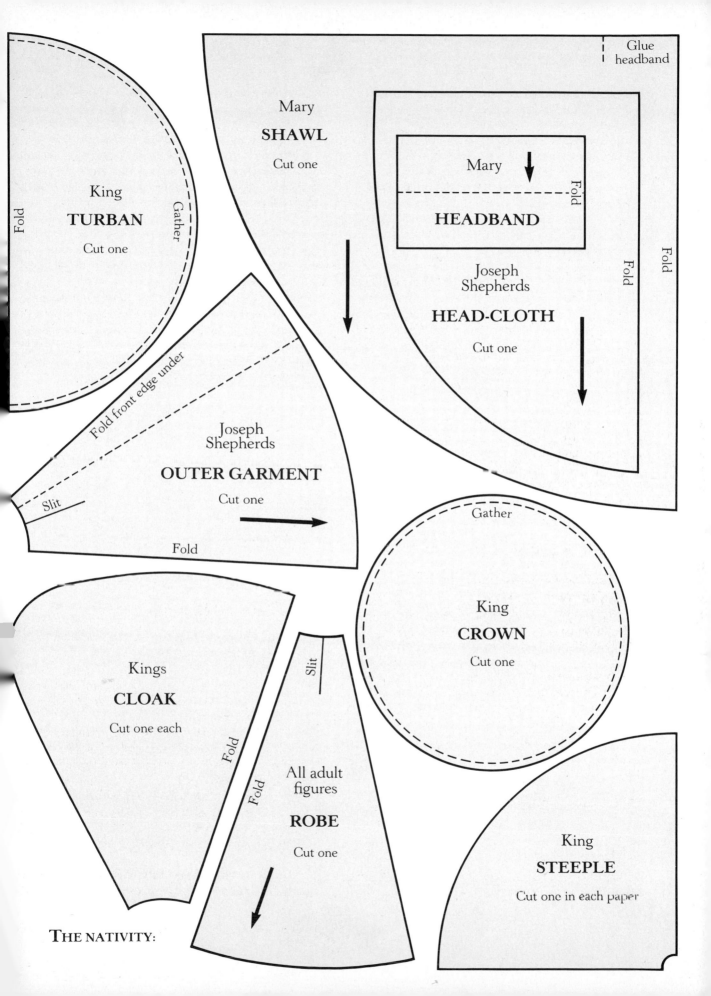

King
TURBAN
Cut one

Fold

Gather

Mary
SHAWL
Cut one

Glue
headband

Mary

HEADBAND

Fold

Fold

Fold

Joseph
Shepherds
HEAD-CLOTH
Cut one

Fold front edge under

Slit

Joseph
Shepherds
OUTER GARMENT
Cut one

Fold

Gather

King
CROWN
Cut one

Kings
CLOAK
Cut one each

Slit

Fold

Fold

All adult
figures
ROBE
Cut one

King
STEEPLE
Cut one in each paper

THE NATIVITY:

neck. Then glue very narrow purchased (or plaited) braid around the inner edge, excluding the neck (this neatens the inside edge, and helps the cloak to stand out dramatically, but isn't essential). Decorate the front corners with stars to match the robe. Fit on the figure, joining the top corners at the centre front.

22 For the hair, tie forty-eight 10cm (4in) lengths of wool loosely at the centre with a single strand. Glue to the top of the head and then to cover the sides and back. Trim the cut ends neatly.

For the black and grey beards, tie twenty 6cm (2½in) lengths of wool tightly at the centre. Fold in half and glue to the centre of the face, as illustrated. Trim to shape. For the white beard, take a piece of stuffing or cotton wool (absorbent cotton) and twist it tightly at the centre; then fold in half and glue it to the face as illustrated.

23 *Green and gold king's turban*: cut the circle in gold felt and gather close to the edge. Put a little stuffing in the centre, then draw it up round the head, drawing the gathers forward so that there are more round the front half of the head than the back; pin into place.

Pin one end of the velvet tubing at the back, then wrap it tightly round the head, gluing it over the gathers and pinning at the centre front (study the illustration for guidance); finish at the back, pinning and gluing over the other cut end. Sew or glue diamanté at the centre front, and surround with a circle of tiny beads.

24 *Violet and gold king's crown*: cut the circle in violet felt and gather close to the edge. Put a little stuffing in the centre, then draw it up round the top of the head; pin into place, distributing the gathers evenly.

Surround the base of the felt with a circle of tiny pearl beads, then pin and glue bands of suitable gold braid immediately above to build up the crown.

25 *Blue and silver king's steeple*: cut the steeple in white paper and foil paper. Curve the white paper round, overlap the straight edges, and glue. Then glue the foil on top. Pin to the head as illustrated.

Pin one end of the velvet tubing at the back, then wrap it twice round the base of the cone, crossing at the front; glue to hold and finish at the back, pinning and gluing over the other cut end. Sew or glue diamanté at the centre front, and surround with a circle of tiny beads.

26 *The Caskets*: the way you create your caskets will depend so much on the beads and bits of glitter you have available that these directions are merely a description of those illustrated, for guidance.

All three caskets are made in the same way, based on approximately 2cm (¾in) diameter coloured glass Christmas tree baubles. A row of narrow silver or gold braid is glued around the centre of the ball (take care with the glue, as it 'lifts' the coloured surface of the bauble). Then two rings of very tiny beads are slipped over the neck of the bauble, and a coloured bead, about 8cm (5/16in) diameter, is glued over the beads, with a tiny pearl right on top.

Pull the arms into an outstretched position, and lean the body backwards slightly. Make sure the casket sits comfortably on the hands; then put a generous blob of glue on each hand, and lower the casket very carefully into place. Don't allow anyone to touch until it's all absolutely dry!

27 Mark round dots for all the characters' eyes, as illustrated (for a soft effect, use a sepia coloured pencil, as described on page 13).

The Nativity Stable and Manger

MATERIALS
2 strips of balsa wood, 90cm (36in) long x 10cm (4in) wide x 3mm (⅛in) thick
Sepia ink or water colour
Dried grass heads (or garden raffia)
Tiny pins
Clear adhesive

1 Cut pieces of balsa as figure 3. Glue the roof pieces together as indicated, to make a piece 25 x 15cm (10 x 6in) for the left side, and 20 x 15cm (8 x 6in) for the right side.

2 Glue and pin the base *between* the side pieces, as figure 4. Glue and pin one horizontal beam level with the *back* edges of the base and sides, resting on the base and between the sides. Glue and pin the second horizontal beam above, level with the top corner of the left side, but 2cm (¾in) below the top corner of the right side (see figure 4).

Glue and pin the vertical beam behind the horizontal ones, the bottom level with lower edge of base.

3 Pin the two roof pieces together, the right side overlapping the left one, as figure 4.

Mark the centre on the top edge of the vertical beam, then place the roof so that it rests on top of both sides, and the angle of the join is level with the marked point on the beam; mark the underside of the roof on the beam (as broken lines on figure 3), then cut off the corners.

Glue and pin the roof into position, overlapping equally at front and back.

4 Mix a wash of ink or paint and water, and paint the whole stable.

5 To make the manger, cut pieces of balsa as in figure 5; two sides, two ends and one base. Glue the ends between the sides, then fit the base inside. Paint with a sepia wash, as step 4. Fill with grass seed heads (or shredded raffia), and rest the Infant Jesus on top.

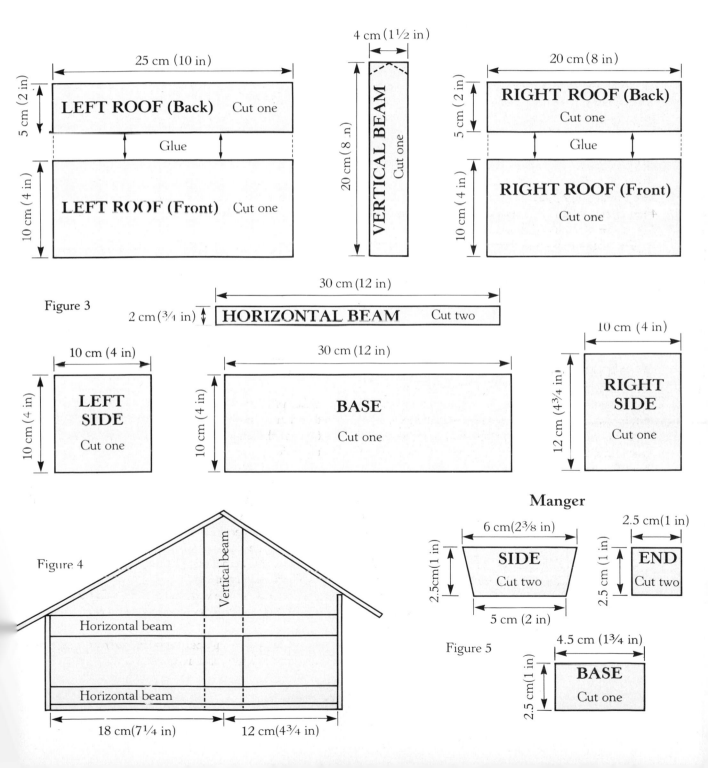

Figure 3

Figure 4

Manger

Figure 5

YOUR VERY OWN
CUDDLY SANTA CLAUS

The most important character on the festive scene, this jolly red-suited Santa could be the focal point of your Christmas decorations. He's incredibly quick and easy to sew from felt. And as he is intended for decorative purposes only, you can cheat and use your pure white polyester filling to make those wonderfully realistic whiskers. Bear in mind that he isn't a toy with a hard life ahead, so just make sure the entire body is adequately stuffed: don't pack the filling too firmly – keep the figure soft and light. (Alternatively, if you *do* want to make the figure as a toy, stuff it more firmly – and make his whiskers from massed loops of thick fluffy knitting yarn. And omit the curtain rings.)

MATERIALS
40cm (½yd) cream felt, 90cm (36in) wide
7cm (2¾in) square of rose pink felt for nose
Scraps (or 2 x 4cm [¾ x ½in]) of black felt
White polyester stuffing
2 brass curtain rings, 20mm (¾in) diameter
Matching threads
Stiff card or plastic (double cereal carton or cottage cheese tub lid) for inner soles
Clear adhesive

Seams: oversew (overcast) the edges to join; approximately 2mm (¹⁄₁₆in) is allowed for seams. Work with right sides together.

1 In cream felt, cut the front head once; cut the back head, the body, outside leg, inside leg and sole twice each (reverse all except the body to cut the second piece); cut the arm four times (reversing two). Cut the nose once in pink felt and the eye twice in black.

Cut the sole twice more, slightly smaller as the broken line, in card or plastic.

2 To make each leg, join the outside and inside leg pieces between A-B to form the centre front seam. Then join C-D for the inside leg seam. Stitch a sole to the lower edge, matching notches and points B and D.

3 Right sides together, join the two legs between E-C-E to form centre front and back seams of lower body.

4 Join the body pieces all round the curved edge, leaving the straight lower (waist) edge open.

Pin the waist edge of the body to the top (waist) edge of the legs, matching notch E to the centre front and back seams. Stitch right across the front, but join only about 3cm (1¼in) at each side of the back, leaving the centre open. Turn to the right side.

5 Push the inner soles down into the feet, temporarily holding them in place from the outside with pins.

Stuff the feet, legs and body adequately but softly; remember, if he's only intended for decoration, he doesn't need to be firmly stuffed like a soft toy. Then slip-stitch neatly across the back to close the waist seam.

6 Join the back head pieces between F-G. Join the back head to the front head all round the curved edge between H and H. Turn to the right side and gather round the straight lower edge with a double thread.

Stuff the head quite firmly, then draw up the gathers until the remaining hole is only about 2cm (¾in) diameter, and secure. Mould and smooth the head between your hands, pushing the sides inwards, to make it nicely rounded.

7 Using a darning needle and double thread, take a stitch through the centre top of the body, from back to front, under the seam: then take a stitch across the hole under the head, from front to back: and then repeat the first stitch through the body. Draw up, so that the head is in the correct position, then repeat the previous stitches to hold it in place. Now ladder stitch (see page 7) all round, alternately taking one stitch through the head and one through the body, securing them firmly together. The best way to do this is to go round once, taking quite large stitches; then, when you have checked everything looks right, go round again, taking smaller stitches and drawing your thread quite taut.

8 To make each arm, join two pieces all round, leaving open between the notches. Turn to the right side and stuff carefully, then slip-stitch the seam to close.

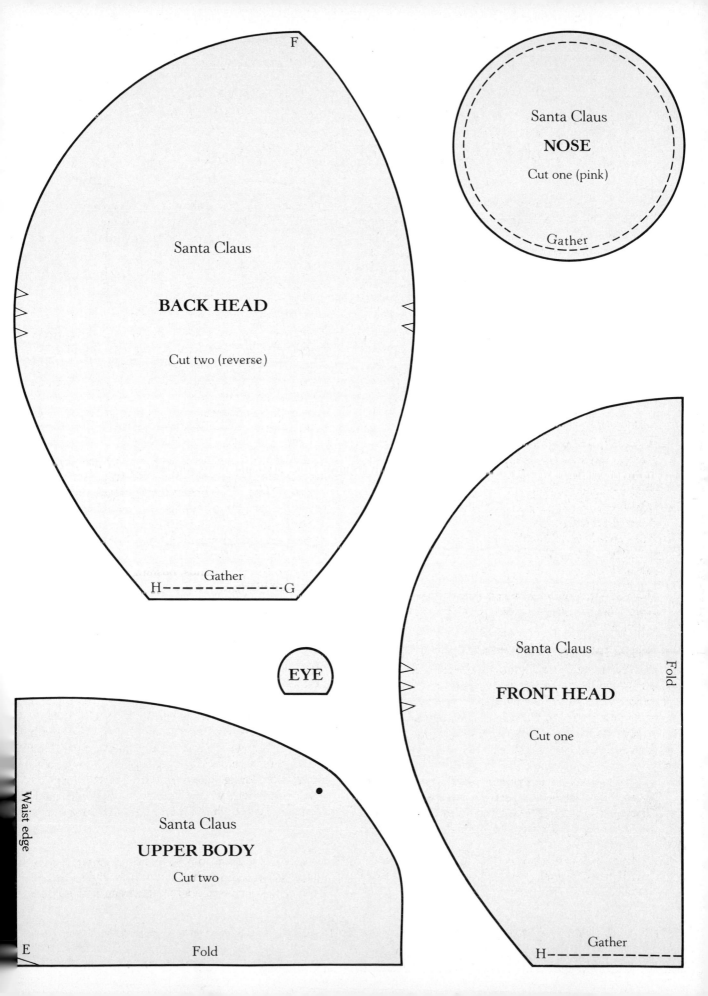

Santa Claus

NOSE

Cut one (pink)

Gather

Santa Claus

BACK HEAD

Cut two (reverse)

F

Gather

H — — — — — — — — — G

EYE

Santa Claus

FRONT HEAD

Cut one

Fold

Gather

H — — — — — — — — —

Waist edge

Santa Claus

UPPER BODY

Cut two

E

Fold

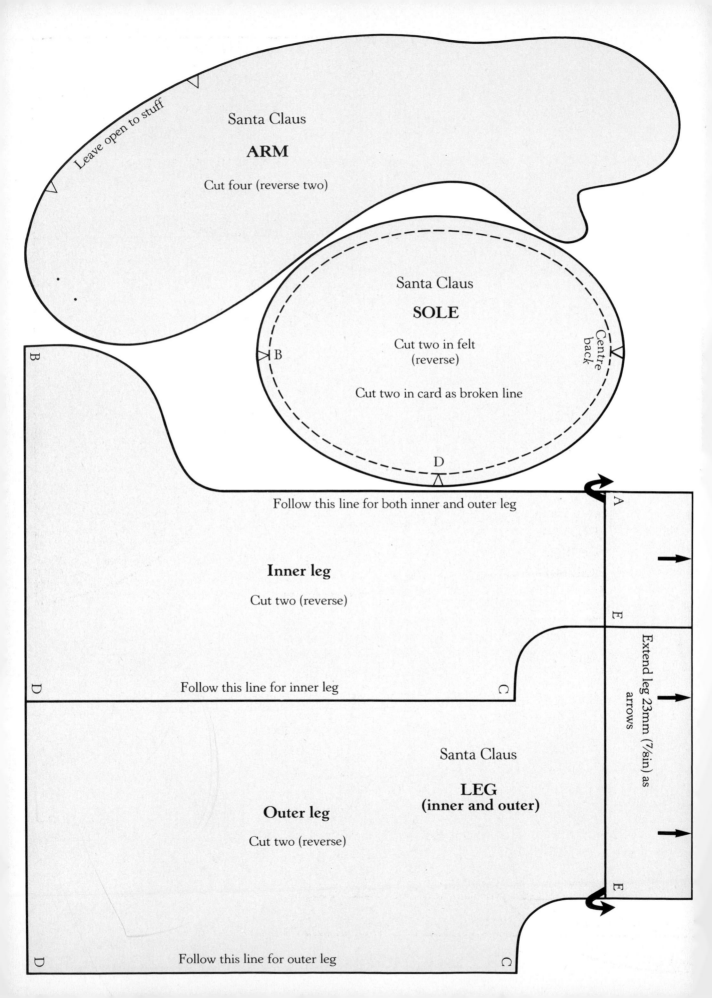

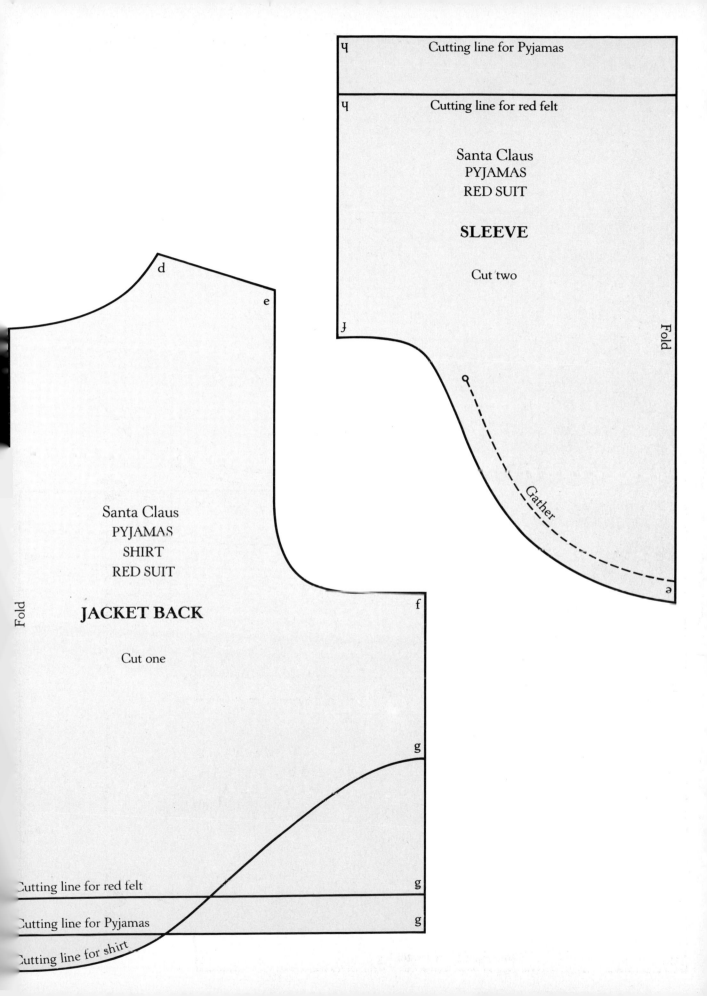

Cutting line for Pyjamas

Cutting line for red felt

Santa Claus
PYJAMAS
RED SUIT

SLEEVE

Cut two

Gather

Fold

d

e

f

Santa Claus
PYJAMAS
SHIRT
RED SUIT

JACKET BACK

Cut one

Fold

g

g

g

Cutting line for red felt

Cutting line for Pyjamas

Cutting line for shirt

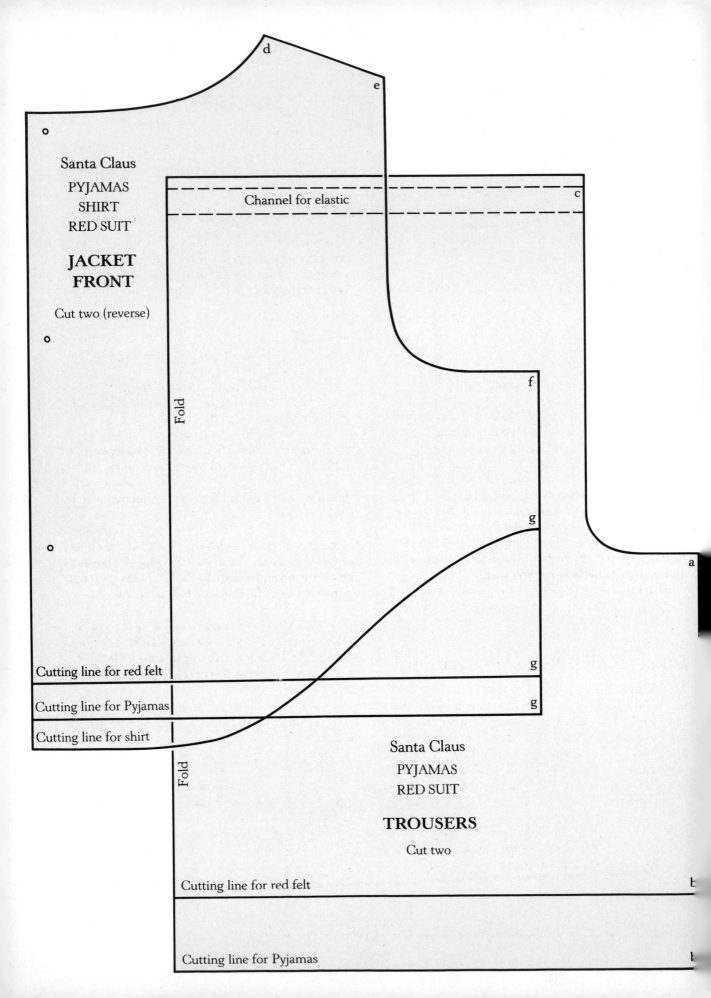

d

e

Santa Claus

PYJAMAS

SHIRT

RED SUIT

**JACKET
FRONT**

Cut two (reverse)

Channel for elastic

c

Fold

f

g

a

Cutting line for red felt

g

Cutting line for Pyjamas

g

Cutting line for shirt

Fold

Santa Claus

PYJAMAS

RED SUIT

TROUSERS

Cut two

Cutting line for red felt

b

Cutting line for Pyjamas

b

Stitch securely to the body at each shoulder, matching the dots; then ladder stitch about 2cm (¾in) across the top.

9 Gather all round the edge of the nose. Partially draw up, then put a small ball of stuffing in the centre before drawing up fully, so that the remaining hole is only about 1cm (⅜in) diameter; then catch the edges together tightly to form a firm round ball.

Stitch to the centre of the face, about 9cm (3½in) below the top seam.

10 Pin the eyes to the face as illustrated. Pin a curtain ring to each side of the nose to check position of eyes and spectacles. When you are satisfied, glue the eyes into place and catch the rings securely to the back of the nose.

11 To make his hair, tease out some polyester filling and place a layer over the back of his head, just overlapping the seam on top, but coming round at each side to form sideburns. When you are satisfied, catch lightly into place with matching thread.

12 To make his whiskers, tease out a piece of filling into an oval shape roughly 25 x 20cm (10 x 8in), making it about half the thickness you want his beard to be; then fold it in half and place the fold across his face, close under the nose. Catch lightly into position with matching thread, then carefully tear off small pieces of filling to shape his beard as you wish.

Wrap thread tightly round the centre of an 8cm (3in) length of filling for his moustache, and sew close under his nose.

Santa's Pyjamas and Nightcap

After a busy working day, Santa needs his sleep. And if you thought he went to bed in his fur-trimmed red suit, you're very much mistaken. He wears striped pyjamas and a nightcap . . . just like everyone else. Nevertheless, his night attire does bear some resemblance to his better-known daytime outfit – which is not so surprising, since both are made from the same pattern.

MATERIALS
60cm (¾yd) medium-weight cotton-type blue-and-white striped fabric, 90cm (36in) wide
25cm (10in) blue bias binding
35cm (14in) narrow round elastic
White double-knit yarn (small amount)
3 snap fasteners
Matching threads
Stiff card, 7cm (2¾in) deep x about 5cm (2in) wide

Seams: approximately 5mm (³⁄₁₆in) is allowed. Except for the waist, don't turn the raw edge under to make a double hem; instead, turn the fabric under once only, and herringbone-stitch over the raw edge.

1 Cut the jacket back and the nightcap (see figure 1) once each; cut the jacket front, sleeve and trousers twice each, reversing the pattern to cut the second piece in each case (watch the stripes to ensure that they match up).

2 Join each trouser leg between a-b. Then, right sides together, join the two pieces between c-a-c, to form centre front and back seams. Clip curves.

Make a hem along the top edge, turning the raw edge under, as broken lines. Then thread elastic through, and draw up to fit the waist.

3 Fit the trousers on the figure and turn up leg hems to length. Herringbone-stitch over the raw edge.

4 Join the jacket (or shirt) back to the front pieces at the shoulders (d-e).

5 Gather the top of each sleeve between the circles, then set into the armholes, matching the side edges (f) and centre top of sleeve to the shoulder seam (e). Draw up the gathers to fit, then stitch. Clip curves.

6 Join the side and sleeve seams (g-f-h). Turn up a hem around the lower edge of the jacket as indicated, and herringbone-stitch. (For the shirt, turn under a very narrow hem around the lower edge.) Turn to the right side.

7 Fit the jacket (or shirt) on the figure and adjust the neckline to fit, if necessary. Turn up the sleeve hems and stitch.

8 Turn under the front edges as broken line and stitch hems. Then bind the neck edge. Stitch snap fasteners to front opening at the points marked o.

9 Right side inside, join the centre back seam of the nightcap as far as the notch (j-k-l); clip the seam at this point, then turn to the right side and complete the seam between l-m.

10 If your fabric is reversible, turn over a 5cm (2in) hem to the *right side* and herringbone-stitch over the raw edge. Then fold over another 5cm (2in) to form turn-back edge of nightcap.

If it is not reversible, turn under a 6cm (2½in) hem and herringbone-stitch over the raw edge. Turn the cap to the right side again and fold the lower edge up 5cm (2in) to form the turn-back edge of the nightcap.

11 To make the tassel, wind yarn evenly thirty times around a 7cm (2¾in) deep piece of card. Slip a 20cm (8in) length of yarn through the loops and tie tightly at one edge; bring the ties down with the other strands. Cut the loops neatly along the other edge. Bind very tightly with white thread about 1cm (⅜in) below the tied top to form head of tassel. Trim the cut ends neatly.

Stitch tassel to point of nightcap, then fold down to hang over his shoulder as illustrated, catching lightly into place at the side of the cap.

Santa's Check Shirt

MATERIALS
20cm (¼yd) red-and-white check gingham, 90cm (36in) wide
25cm (10in) red or white bias binding
3 snap fasteners
Matching thread

Seams: as for the pyjamas.

1 Using the patterns for the jacket, cut the back once and the front twice (note cutting line for lower edge on both – and reverse pattern to cut second front piece). Cut the separate shirt sleeve twice.

2 Follow the directions for his pyjamas, steps 4-8 inclusive.

Santa's Red Suit and Cap

Santa's working outfit is made from warm red felt, so it's even quicker and easier to make than his pyjamas, because there are no raw edges. Many shops stock fur trimming by the metre/yard, so you may prefer to use this. But the method described below is very simple, and extremely effective. It doesn't matter whether you cut the fur across the width of the fabric or lengthwise; the advantage of cutting it lengthways is that you can follow the lines on the back.

MATERIALS
40cm (½yd) red felt, 90cm (36in) wide
25cm (¼yd) x 60cm (24in) white fur fabric (see above)
50cm (½yd) black grosgrain ribbon, 23mm (1in) wide
2.5cm (1in) silver (or gilt) buckle
White double-knit yarn (or purchased pompon)
Thin card (if making pompon)
3 snap fasteners
Matching threads
35cm (14in) narrow round elastic

Seams: oversew (overcast) the edges to join; approximately 2mm (¹/₁₆in) is allowed for seams. Work with right sides together. Press seams flat by drawing your thumbnail along them before turning to the right side.

1 Cut the jacket back and the cap (see figure 1) once each (note higher cutting lines on both); cut the jacket front, sleeve and trousers twice each, reversing the pattern to cut the second front piece (again, note higher cutting lines).

2 Join each trouser leg between a-b. Then, right sides together, join the two pieces between c-a-c, to form centre front and back seams.

Turn the top edge over to the wrong side and make a 1cm (⅜in) hem. Thread elastic through and draw up to fit waist.

3 Cut two strips of fur fabric, each 4cm (1½in) wide x 35cm (14in) long. Fold each in half lengthways, wrong side inside; oversew the raw edges together, making long stitches which take up only the very edge of the fabric (figure 2). Now flatten the strip so that the seam falls in the centre (this will be the back of the trimming – figure 3); return along the seam, this time making long running stitches which catch up just enough of the underneath (front) fabric to keep the trimming flat.

Pin the fur strips round the lower edge of the trouser legs, overlapping the ends; join the ends, then stitch the trimming into place from the inside.

4 Join the jacket back to the front pieces at the shoulders (d-e).

5 Gather the top of each sleeve *close to the edge* between the circles, then set into the armholes, matching the side edges (f) and the centre top of the sleeve to the shoulder seam (e). Draw up the gathers to fit, then stitch.

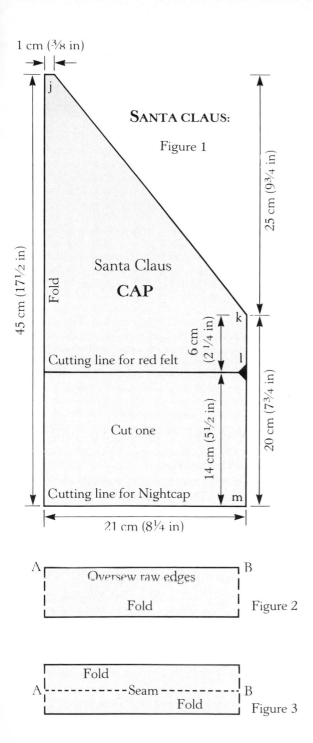

1 cm (³/₈ in)

SANTA CLAUS:

Figure 1

25 cm (9¾ in)

45 cm (17½ in)

Fold

Santa Claus

CAP

Cutting line for red felt

6 cm (2¼ in)

k

l

Cut one

14 cm (5½ in)

20 cm (7¾ in)

Cutting line for Nightcap

m

21 cm (8¼ in)

A ———— Oversew raw edges ———— B

Fold

Figure 2

Fold

A — — — — Seam — — — — B

Fold

Figure 3

6 Join the side and sleeve seams (g-f-h)

7 Turn under the front edges as shown by broken line, and stitch hems. Turn to the right side.

8 Cut a strip of fur fabric 4cm (1½in) wide x 25cm (10in) long. Prepare it as step 3, then stitch it round

the neck edge to form a stand-up collar; oversew the ends neatly.

9 Prepare two more strips of fur, 4cm (1½in) wide x 25cm (10in) long, and trim the sleeves. Trim the lower edge of the jacket with another strip, 50cm (20in) long.

10 Stitch snap fasteners to front opening at points marked o.

11 Fix the buckle to one end of the ribbon to make his belt; catch the corners at the other end of the ribbon together underneath to form a neat point. Fit round waist.

12 Join the centre back seam of the cap (j-k-l). Turn to the right side.
   Cut a strip of fur fabric 8cm (3in) wide x 50cm (20in) long. Pin round the bottom of the cap, right sides together; trim to length and join the short ends of the fur, then oversew together round the lower edge. Turn the fur to the wrong side, folding it length-ways along the centre, then slip-stitch the other edge inside the cap.

13 Make a woolly pompon (see Finishing Touches), cutting your card circles 5cm (2in) diameter. Stitch to point of the cap, then fold down to hang over his shoulder as illustrated, catching it lightly into place at the side of the cap.

Santa's Black Boots

MATERIALS
14cm (5½in) black felt, 90cm (36in) wide
Black thread

1 Cut the boot and sole twice each.

2 To make each boot, oversew the centre front seam between the notch and toe. Then turn to the right side and join the remainder of the seam between the notch and top edge. Turn to the wrong side again.

3 Matching the centre back and front and the notches, stitch a sole round the lower edge. Turn to the right side.

4 Fold the top edge over twice, as shown by broken lines; catch lightly at the front and back to hold the cuff in place.

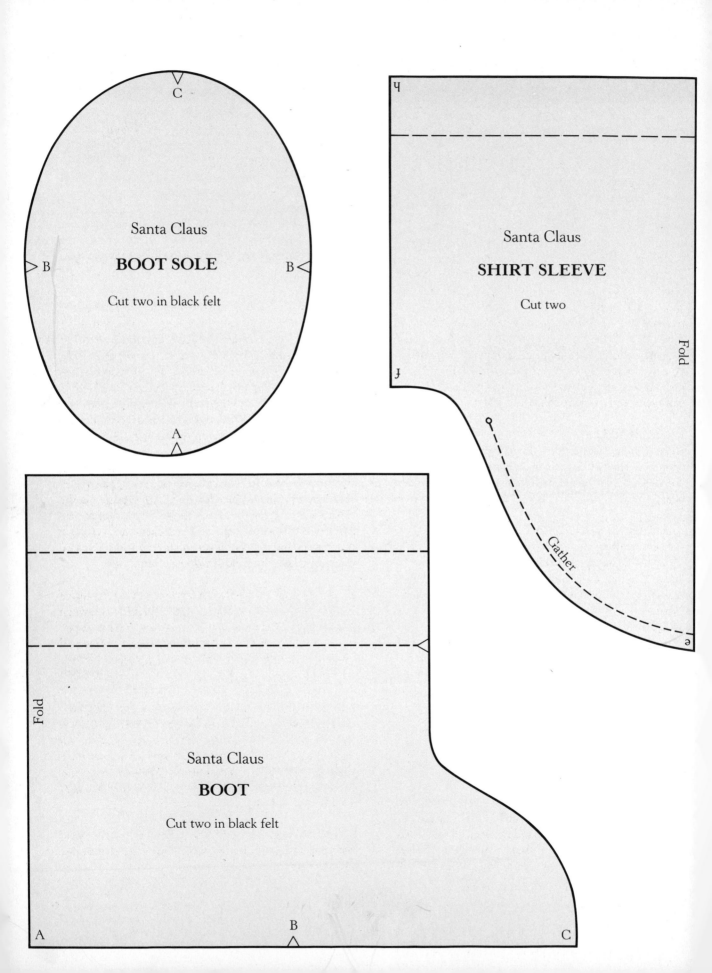

Santa Claus

BOOT SOLE

Cut two in black felt

Santa Claus

SHIRT SLEEVE

Cut two

Fold

Gather

Fold

Santa Claus

BOOT

Cut two in black felt

SEVEN CHRISTMAS STOCKING BEARS
How to make and dress one and all

Quick to make – and even quicker to sell. Make him in a soft, thick fur, in any shade you please. Being such a busy bear, he needs his workmanlike dungarees and cap. But if you're planning a more leisurely bear – perhaps for a new baby – he's just as adorable in his birthday suit.

The features are felt; cheap and very easy to do. But you can, if you prefer, use a purchased nose and eyes; just make sure they have safety washers, so that they can be locked in from behind.

MATERIALS
30cm (12in) fur fabric, 90cm (36in) wide
Scraps (or 4cm [1½in] square) of black felt
20cm (¼yd) felt, 90cm (36in) wide, for dungarees and cap
60cm (¾yd) grosgrain ribbon, 23mm (1in) wide, for dungarees
45cm (½yd) black braid, 10mm (⅜in) wide, for cap
Polyester stuffing
25cm (10in) narrow round elastic, for dungarees
30cm (12in) narrow round elastic, for hat
Stranded black embroidery cotton
Matching and black threads
Medium-weight card (cereal carton)
Stiff card or plastic (double cereal carton or cottage cheese tub lid)
Dry-stick adhesive (optional)
Clear adhesive

Seams: on fur fabric, approximately 5mm (³⁄₁₆in) is allowed for seams; sew with a back stitch, using double thread, if you like. To join felt, oversew the edges; approximately 2mm (¹⁄₁₆in) is allowed for seams. Work with right sides together unless otherwise instructed.

1 In fur fabric, cut the head gusset once; cut the face (reversing one), the body/leg and the sole twice each; cut the arm (reversing two) and the ear (note direction of pile) four times each. Mark notches and circles. Leave the face pattern pinned to the fabric. Cut the

sole again slightly smaller, following the broken line, in card or stiff plastic.

2 For a smiling bear, mark the mouth very carefully on both face pieces. To do this, stick a pin straight down through the pattern and fabric every 3mm (⅛in) or so; push the heads right down against the paper, then gently ease the pattern away to leave the pins stuck in the fabric. Using black sewing thread, back-stitch along this line, following the position of the pins very accurately and removing them as you sew (make sure your stitches show clearly on the right side).

3 Join the two pieces between A-B, making sure the two mouth lines meet exactly. Using six strands of embroidery cotton, embroider over the mouth on the right side in stem (outline) stitch. If you prefer, you can leave this until step 15, when the bear is stuffed; but the sewing is easier if you do it now – and it is also easier to make the mouth a good, even shape.

4 Carefully match the tip of the gusset (A) to the top of the seam; then join it to each side of the face between A-C. Accuracy is very important around the nose area; before *each stitch* match the raw edges of the face and gusset, taking care not to stretch either piece of fabric.

Join the gusset dart (D-E). Turn to the right side.

5 Stuff the head quite firmly, pushing the filling well up into the nose and chin. Using a double thread, gather round the lower edge of the head, then draw up tightly and secure, leaving just a small hole no more than 2cm (¾in) in diameter (before securing your thread, check that the head is sufficiently stuffed, adding a little more filling under the chin).

6 Join an arm to each side of both body pieces, between F-G. Right sides facing, join the two pieces together between J-K-J.

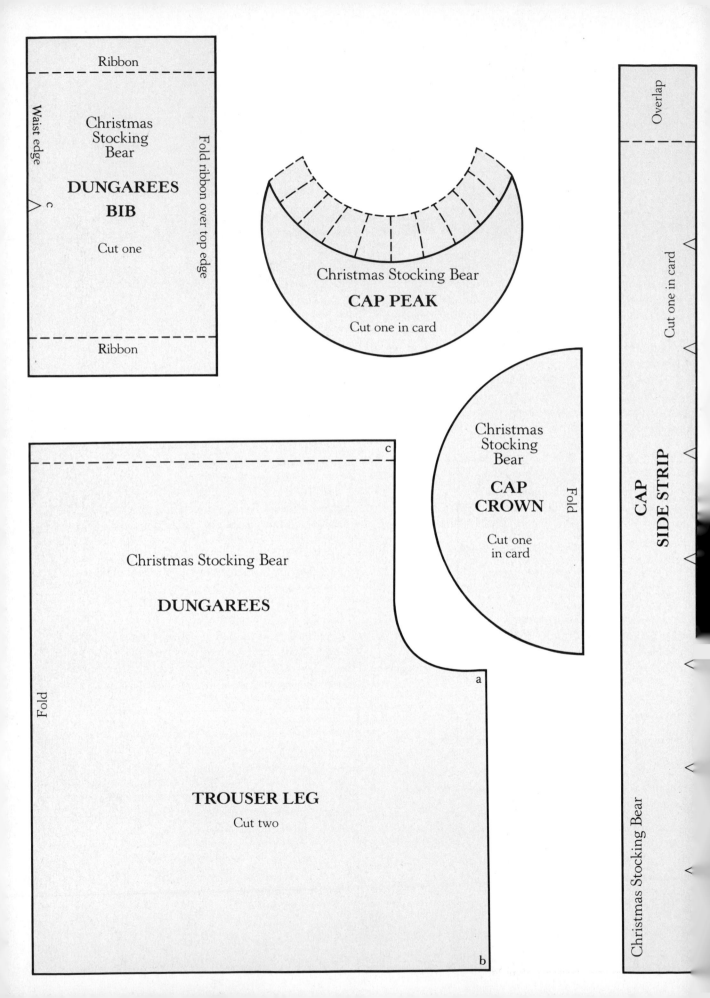

Ribbon

Waist edge

Christmas
Stocking
Bear

**DUNGAREES
BIB**

Cut one

c

Fold ribbon over top edge

Ribbon

Christmas Stocking Bear

CAP PEAK

Cut one in card

Christmas
Stocking
Bear

**CAP
CROWN**

Cut one
in card

Fold

Overlap

Cut one in card

**CAP
SIDE STRIP**

Christmas Stocking Bear

c

Christmas Stocking Bear

DUNGAREES

Fold

a

TROUSER LEG

Cut two

b

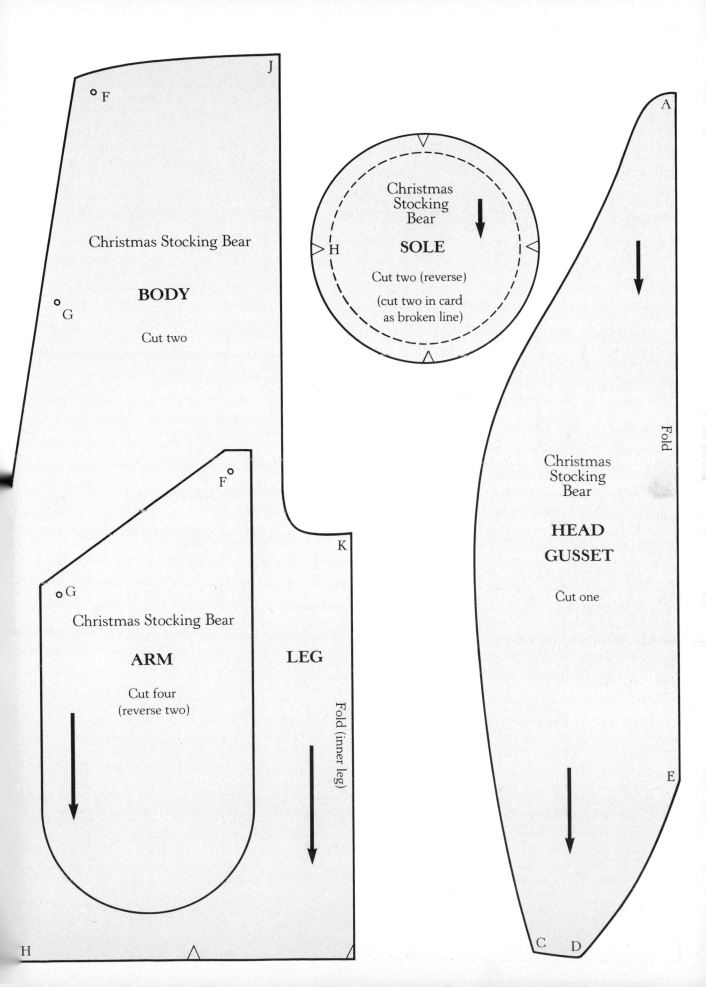

7 Fold each half along the leg fold line, right side in-side, and join all round the arm and down the side of the body and leg – from F to H.

8 Matching notches and point H, *oversew* a sole to the bottom of each leg, making sure the pile runs in the same direction on both.

9 Turn under and tack a narrow hem around the top edges of the body. Turn to the right side.

10 Push card or plastic soles into the feet and hold in position temporarily with pins from the outside.

11 Stuff quite firmly, pushing the filling well down into the feet and paws. Then slip-stitch the edges to-gether round the top of the body (adding a little more stuffing, if necessary, before finally closing the seam).

12 Using a darning needle and double thread, take a stitch through the centre top of the body, from back to front, under the seam; then take a stitch across the hole under the head, from front to back; and then repeat the first stitch through the body. Draw up, so that the head is in the correct position, then repeat the previous stitches to hold it in place. Now ladder stitch (see page 7) all round, alternately taking one stitch through the head and one through the body, securing them firmly together. The best way to do this is to go round once, taking quite large stitches; then, when you have checked everything looks right, go round again, taking smaller stitches and drawing your thread taut.

13 To make each ear, *oversew* two pieces together all round, leaving the straight lower edge open. Turn to the right side. Pin raw edges together, then gather across the bottom of the ear and draw up to measure about 5cm (2in), so ear curves attractively.

14 Pin the ears to the top of the head, the inner corners overlapping the gusset about 1cm (3/8in). When you are satisfied with their position, ladder stitch into place at both front and back.

15 Cut the eyes and nose in black felt (see page 6: cutting circles). Glue the nose to the tip of the gusset, then pin eyes to face, following illustrations; move them about until you are satisfied, then glue.

16 In felt, cut the dungarees leg twice, and the bib and cap once each. In medium weight card, cut the cap crown, side strip and peak (ignore broken lines) once each. Transfer all markings carefully.

17 To make the dungarees, fold each leg piece in half as the pattern and join a-b. Then join the two pieces, right sides together, between c-a-c, to form the centre front and back seams.

18 Fold the wide ribbon lengthways over the top edge of the bib, and bind neatly. Then cut the remaining ribbon in half for the straps; pin them so that half the width of the ribbon overlaps the side edges of the bib, cut ends of ribbon level with the lower edge of the bib, and the remaining ribbon extending at the top. Stitch.

19 Matching the notch (c) to the centre front seam, place the bib over the trousers, right sides together and waist edges matching; stitch together (don't over-sew), making a 5mm (1/4in) seam.

Turn over a 5mm (1/4in) hem around the remaining top edge of the trousers (broken line), and stitch. Thread elastic through and draw up to fit waist, secur-ing the cut ends at each side of the bib.

20 Fit dungarees on bear. Take the straps over his shoulders and cross at the back; tuck ends of ribbon down inside trousers and stitch at the waist to hold.

21 To make his cap, curve the side strip round into a circle and glue the overlap. Then glue the card crown to the wrong side of the felt circle, as broken line on pattern (use a glue-stick to do this, if you have one).

Gather all around the edge, then place the felt circle over the side strip, the cut edge of the felt level with the lower edge of the card circle, and pin at each notch; draw up gathers to fit closely and oversew together all round the lower edge of the side strip.

22 Glue one side of the peak to the felt and cut the felt level all round. Then glue the underside to felt, but trim only the outer edge level; allow a surplus around the inner edge as broken line on pattern. Snip the over-lapping felt to form tabs, as indicated. Very carefully glue these tabs up inside the lower edge of the cap.

23 Glue braid around the peak, folding it over the edge. Then glue braid around lower edge of cap, over the gathers (join at back).

24 Fix ends of elastic inside cap at each side, so that it fits snugly under his chin.

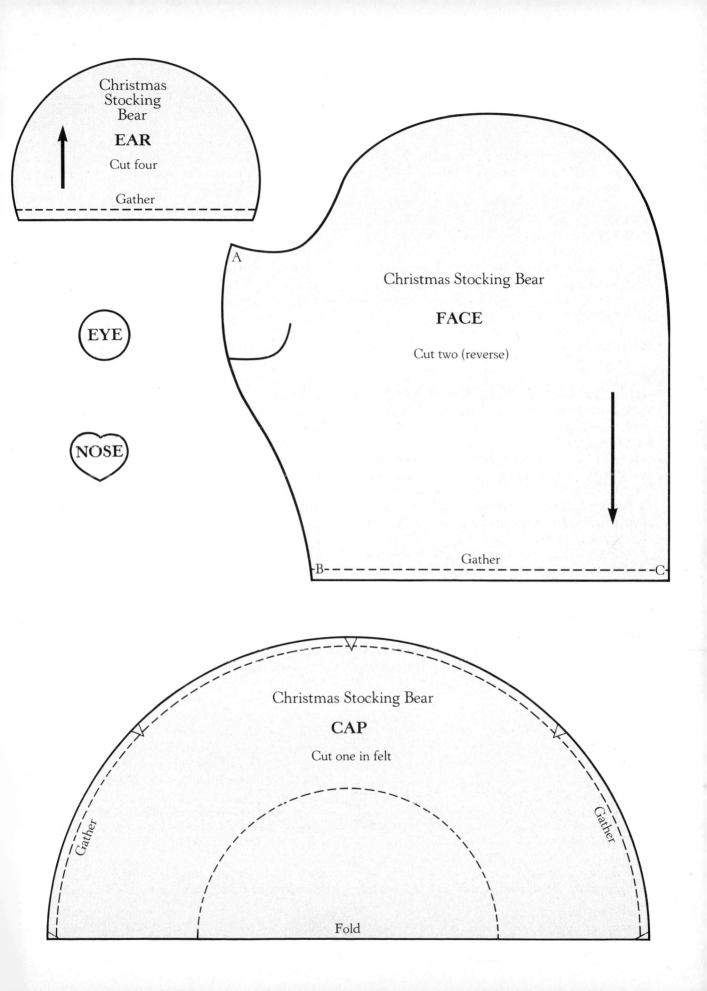

Christmas
Stocking
Bear

EAR

Cut four

Gather

EYE

NOSE

A

Christmas Stocking Bear

FACE

Cut two (reverse)

B Gather C

Christmas Stocking Bear

CAP

Cut one in felt

Gather

Gather

Fold

ANGELICA, THE CHRISTMAS MOUSE

Although she creates a disturbance in Santa's workshop, the Christmas Mouse has a very sweet nature. This attractive little creature makes an unusual decoration at Christmas-time. Or a charming gift, to stand on a dressing table or beside the sewing machine, where Angelica becomes a helpful pincushion.

MATERIALS

15cm (6in) square of mid-brown felt
6cm (2½in) square of cream felt
Scrap of black felt
20cm (8in) square of white felt
Polyester stuffing
12 x 40cm (4¾ x 16in) pale blue spotted voile (dotted Swiss) or similar lightweight fabric
40cm (15in) white lace, 10mm (⅜in) deep, for petticoat
40cm (15in) very narrow white lace, to trim dress
30cm (12in) white lace, 20mm (¾in) deep, for collar
Small pearl beads for circlet
2 small black domed sequins (optional)
Small silver flower sequin (optional)
Black stranded embroidery cotton
3 pipe cleaners (chenille stems): one 16.5 (6½in) long; two 10cm (4in) long
Circle of stiff card (double cereal carton), 7.5cm (3in) in diameter
Clear adhesive

Seams: oversew (overcast) with tiny stitches to join felt. Make 5mm (³⁄₁₆in) seams on fabric. Work with right sides together.

Patterns: where a FOLD is indicated, cut in folded *paper*, then open out to cut in single thickness felt.

1 In brown felt, cut the head gusset and tail once each; cut the face twice (reversing the pattern to cut the second piece), and the paw four times. Cut the ear twice in cream felt, then glue to brown felt and cut level with the edge of the cream felt.

In white felt, cut the body once and the arm four

times. Glue the card circle to the felt, then cut the felt a bare 3mm (⅛in) outside the edge of the card.

In fabric, cut the dress once and the sleeve twice.

2 Join the face pieces between A-B. Fit the tip of the gusset (A) behind the top of the seam at A and oversew carefully to each side of the face from A to C. Stitch the dart D-E. Turn head to the right side.

3 Cut the body pattern along the broken line. Pin the smaller top section to the body felt, and run a double gathering thread level with the edge of the pattern, marking the waistline; don't draw up, but leave the loose thread on the *right* side of the felt. Remove the pattern.

4 Join the centre back seam, leaving open between the notches for the tail. Mark the top edge equally into four, then gather. Push the head down inside and, right sides together, pin round the neck edge, matching points B and D at the centre front and back respectively, and the notches at each side. Draw up the gathers to fit and oversew together. Turn to the right side.

5 Stuff the head very firmly, moulding it into shape from outside.

6 Bend the longer pipe cleaner in half and wrap some stuffing round it, beginning with a small amount at the tip (the bend) and increasing a little towards the ends.

Gather the narrow end of the tail (F-F); draw up tightly and turn to the right side. Fit the covered pipe cleaner inside, pushing the tip well up into the gathers, and slip-stitch the seam between F-G.

With the seam towards the body, bend the tail as illustrated and fit the end inside the body, stitching it securely into place.

7 Mark the lower edge of the body equally into four, then gather. Mark the edges of the base into four. With wrong sides together (card inside), pin the base

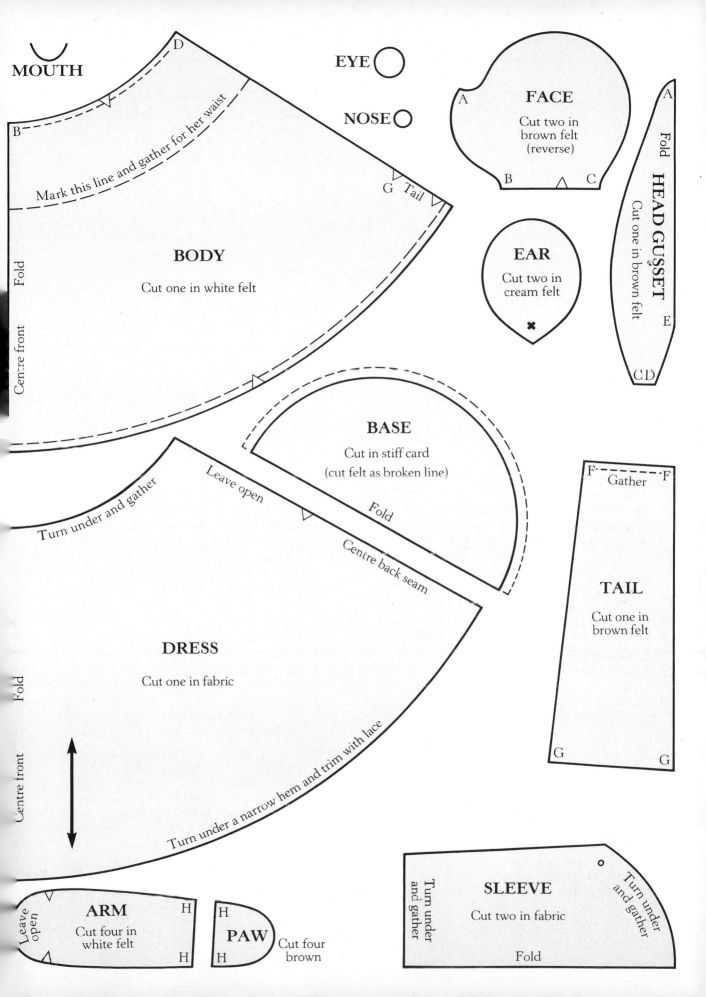

MOUTH

EYE

NOSE ◯

FACE
Cut two in
brown felt
(reverse)

A

B C

HEAD GUSSET
Cut one in brown felt

Fold

A

E

CD

EAR
Cut two in
cream felt

✗

D

B

Mark this line and gather for her waist

BODY
Cut one in white felt

Fold

Centre front

G Tail

BASE
Cut in stiff card
(cut felt as broken line)

Fold

Centre back seam

Turn under and gather

Leave open

TAIL
Cut one in
brown felt

F F
Gather

G G

DRESS
Cut one in fabric

Fold

Centre front

Turn under a narrow hem and trim with lace

ARM
Cut four in
white felt

Leave open

H

H

PAW
Cut four
brown

H

H

SLEEVE
Cut two in fabric

Turn under
and gather

Turn under
and gather

Fold

to the body, matching marked points. Draw up the gathers to fit, distributing them evenly, and oversew neatly together around three-quarters of the base. Stuff the body firmly, then slip-stitch the opening.

8 Draw up the waistline gathers tightly and secure.

9 Stitch a paw to the lower edge of each arm (H-H). Then join two pieces together for each arm, leaving open at the top between the notches. Turn to the right side and push a little stuffing into each paw.

Bend the two remaining pipe cleaners in half and wrap a little stuffing round each. Fit one inside each arm, adding more stuffing around them. Slip-stitch the top edges together.

10 Gather the petticoat lace, then pin it equally round the body, lower edges level; draw up, distributing the gathers evenly, and stitch into place, finishing the ends neatly at each side of the tail.

11 Join the centre back seam of the dress below the notch; turn under and tack the seam at each side above the notch.

Turn under a very narrow hem around the lower edge, then trim with narrow lace. Turn under the narrowest possible hem around the neck, and gather close to the edge.

Fit dress on mouse; catch the top corners together at the back and draw up the gathers around the neck. Slip-stitch centre back opening neatly. Gather lace and draw up round neck.

12 To make each sleeve, join the side seam as far as the circle. Turn up a narrow hem around the wrist edge and gather, leaving the loose thread on the outside. Turn to the right side and fit an arm inside, with the sleeve seam *between* the two arm seams. Draw up the gathers tightly around the wrist. Stitch (or stick) lace around the wrists as illustrated.

Turn the top edge of the sleeve under and gather close to the edge: draw up tightly and secure.

13 Stitch the top of each arm to the side of the body, about 5mm (¼in) below the neck edge of the dress.

Bend the arms at the elbows and stitch the paws together.

14 Dab a spot of adhesive at X on the cream side of each ear, then pinch tightly together until firmly glued. Pin to each side of the head, moving around until you are satisfied (study the illustration for guidance), then glue into position.

15 Cut the eyes and nose in black felt. Glue a black sequin in the centre of each eye. Glue the nose over the tip of the gusset, then pin the eyes at each side, lower edges of eyes and nose almost level; move the eyes around until you are satisfied, then glue in place.

Mark the shape of the mouth with pins; the upper corners are 1cm (⅜in) apart, and the centre is 5mm (³⁄₁₆in) below the nose. Then embroider in stem (outline) stitch, using three strands of embroidery cotton.

16 Thread a string of pearl beads and knot the ends to make a 2cm (¾in) diameter circle; glue to the top of the head as illustrated.

17 Glue a flower sequin to the tip of the tail as illustrated, if liked.

A Cloak for Angelica

A cosy cloak to keep the Christmas Mouse warm as toast on cold winter nights. Make your own fur edging from a piece of white fur fabric, preferably with a fairly short pile. Simply follow the lines on the back to cut 2cm (¾in) wide strips, joining them together as necessary.

MATERIALS
23 x 45cm (9 x 18in) blue felt
1m (1⅛yd) white fur trimming, 2cm (¾in) wide (see above)
30cm (12in) satin ribbon, 3mm (⅛in) wide, for ties
Matching threads

1 Cut the cloak and hood (overleaf) once each. Transfer the markings carefully.

2 Gather the neck edge of the cloak and draw up to measure 10cm (4in).

3 Gather the straight edge of the hood. Pin the neck edge of the cloak, matching notches. Draw up the gathers to fit, distributing them evenly between the pins, and oversew (overcast) the two gathered edges together. Turn to the right side.

4 Gather the curved edge of the hood and draw up to measure 15cm (6in).

5 Cut strips of fur as above; mark a pencil line down the centre on the back.

6 Stitch fur all round the edge of the cloak on the right side, half the fur overlapping the edge of the felt. Then turn the overlap over to the inside and stitch neatly.

7 Trim the edge of the hood in the same way, but first mark a 15cm (6in) length of fur equally into eight; then pin to the hood matching the marked points to the notches. Distribute the gathers evenly between the pins as you stitch the fur into place.

8 Cut the ribbon in half and stitch one piece at each side of the neck, for ties.

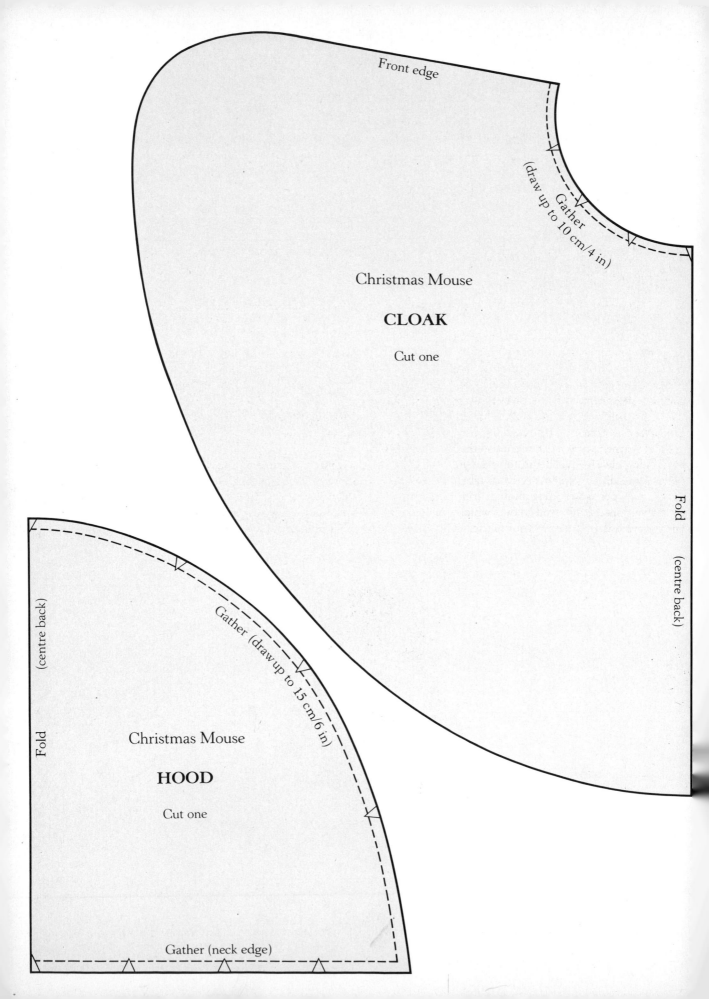

Front edge

Gather (draw up to 10 cm/4 in)

Christmas Mouse

CLOAK

Cut one

Fold (centre back)

Fold (centre back)

Gather (draw up to 15 cm/6 in)

Fold

Christmas Mouse

HOOD

Cut one

Gather (neck edge)

THE BEARS' CHRISTMAS STOCKING
Just as you fancy

There's only one rule when you make the Christmas stocking: you're not allowed to *buy* any of the materials! Most people should be able to find everything they need amongst all those bags and boxes of lovingly stored odds and ends.

First, decide on the fabric you are going to use; this can be the same both sides, or you can have two contrasting ones (but they should be a similar weight). Then find a suitable strip of felt for the cuff (again, this can be different on each side). Make up the stocking as described below (steps 1 and 2). Now tip out all your bits of lace, ribbon, braid, beads, sequins . . . even flowers and feathers. Spread them out so that you can see everything clearly, and begin to make your selection, placing the different items on your fabric to see how they look – perhaps adding another trimming on top of the first one. Try to find colours which match, tone with or echo the colours in your fabric.

MATERIALS

2 pieces of fabric, each 35 x 28cm (14 x 11in), for the stocking
2 pieces of felt, each 3 x 20cm (1¼ x 8in), for the cuff
15cm (6in) lengths of each trimming (for horizontal bands)
Additional decoration as above
90cm (1yd) ric-rac braid, narrow lace, or other trimming to edge the stocking (see illustration)
50cm (½yd) fancy ribbon, 23mm (1in) wide, for bow (optional)
Matching threads
Clear adhesive

1 Trace the pattern (overleaf) and cut it out. Pin the pattern on the right side of one piece of fabric, and draw round it with a contrasting pencil or chalk, in order to leave a clear line. Then cut it out – about 1cm (⅜in) beyond the marked line.

CHRISTMAS STOCKING

2 Turn the raw top edge over to the *right* side and stitch. Cut the cuff in felt and either glue or stitch it across the top, but don't join the short ends yet.

3 Now it's all yours to design and do as you please. Decide the trimmings you are going to use, and how you are going to place them, as described above. Don't fix anything permanently until you have experimented with different arrangements; pin the pieces to the stocking, so that you can keep moving them around until you are happy. Just make sure that the cut ends of each band of trimming are level with the marked line at each side.

When you are satisfied, stitch and/or glue the pieces into position; before doing so, it's usually a good idea to rule horizontal lines across the stocking, for guidance.

4 Pin the decorated stocking to the second piece of fabric, wrong sides together. Cut the backing fabric level with the first piece, allowing extra at the top.

5 Turn the top edge over and make a cuff for the second side, as step 2.

6 Join the two pieces by stitching along the marked line.

7 Trim off the straight cut edge all round the stocking with pinking shears.

8 Stitch or glue ric-rac braid, lace or alternative trimming all round the stocking, over the stitching line.

9 Trim off the ends of the cuff neatly and glue them together at each side.

10 Tie a bow at the centre of a 50cm (½yd) length of ribbon and stitch to the top of the stocking, if required.

INDEX